There is Nothing New Under the Sun

The Biblical History of Climate Change and Atomic Destruction in the Beginning

Son of Yahweh

7/21/2013

Let all the nations be gathered together, and let the people be assembled: who among them can declare this, and show us former things? Let them bring forth their witnesses, that they may be justified: or let them hear, and say, it is truth. Isaiah 43:9

There is Nothing New Under the Sun

Table of Contents

Written by
Yibniyah Hawkins
5/27/2013

Introduction

This work introduces mankind to an ancient history that began before the earth and the visible heaven (the Milky Way) existed. The reader will learn about the undertaking of a assembly of heavenly beings who rebelled against the universal laws of peace. They had for millions of years lived without the curses one brings into his life once he deviates from the laws of peace. They began to doubt Yahweh who guided them for millions of years away from the curses they are now experiencing. The effects of sin had never being fully realized, until the undertaking to practice sin in rebellion to Yahweh instruction began. The forewarning of the destruction they would bring into the lives Yahweh warned them of was perceived as alleged possibilities. There was no historical evidence to validate the doubtful imprecations Yahweh predicted would come into their lives. They practice a way of life which consisted of the mixer of righteousness and evil. Yahweh in his love for his creation developed a plan to prove what he was warning them of. In this ancient time period he created the earth and the visible heavens (the Milky Way) for the purpose of his plan to allow these (gods) to practice a way of life which consisted of the mixer of righteousness and evil. The plan was to document all the curses that would develop from living this way of life. These gods for many years adhere too many of Yahweh's laws of peace, but as time pass practicing this new way of life Yahweh warned them of, the curses in their lives became a true reality. The laws of peace were misused and neglected in there pursuit for peace and happiness. The earth and the visible heavens became a battle ground in there lust for power and control over each other. The Government of Peace began to record all the curses that naturally resulted from this way of life wars, sexual perversion, the inventing of weapons of mass destruction and the

Written by
Yibniyah Hawkins
5/27/2013

destruction of both heavens and earth. These events are documented for us in the Holy Scripture as former events, that Yahweh commands us to remember. The results of this Great Experiment he used to guide his plan of salvation for all creation. These former events moved Yahweh to create a family of men and women who he is making in his likeness and image to guide creation away from sin and death. Mankind is now experience the same way of life and the curses this way of life brings. The plan of salvation as the reader will learn was fashion according to the events that take place in an ancient time. Yahweh permitted this way of life symbolized as the fruit of a tree to which Eve was tempted into partaking of to be introduced to mankind. This way of life presented to Eve was the "original undertaking to sin" that was initiated in the Universe.

And the woman said unto the serpent, we may eat of the fruit of the trees of the garden: But of the fruit of the tree which *is* in the midst of the garden, Yahweh has said, you shall not eat of it, neither shall you touch it, are you will die. And the serpent said unto the woman, you shall not surely die: For He knows that in the day you eat thereof, then your eyes shall be opened, and ***you shall be as gods, knowing righteousness and evil.***

Gen 3:2-5 (KJV)

Yibniyah Hawkins, Author

Eyes on the Truth.......

Written by
Yibniyah Hawkins
5/27/2013

Chapter One

Declaring the End from the Beginning

The growing threat of nuclear war now escalating amongst the nation prompted me to write about an ancient history hidden in the Holy Scripture for thousands of years. This history reveals the reason for Yahweh establishing a plan to save the universe and all creation from destruction. This work will reveal the history of both the heavens and the earth, before man was placed on it to fulfill a part of Yahweh plan to create from man moral leaders like him. These leaders will rid the earth and the heavens from sin and the curses sin brings. Yahweh who all the prophets show in their writings loves all creation, and designed a plan to save it from the corruption it is now undergoing. The prophet Isaiah was inspired to write concerning one of the great secrets concerning Yahweh's plan hidden in words inspired to be written under the direction of the Holy Spirit. Notice with me the following scripture:

 Remember the former things of old: for I *am* Yahweh, and *there is* none else; *I am* Yahweh, and *there is* none like me, ***Declaring the end from the beginning, and from ancient times the things that are not yet done, saying, My counsel shall stand, and I will fulfill all my plan:*** Calling a ravenous bird from the east, the man that executes my counsel from a far country: yea, I have spoken *it*, I will also bring it to pass; I have purposed *it*, I will also do it. Hearken unto me, you stubborn-hearted, which *are* far from righteousness: I bring near my righteousness; it shall not be far off, and my salvation shall not tarry: and I will place salvation in Zion for Israel my glory.

Written by
Yibniyah Hawkins
5/27/2013

There is Nothing New Under the Sun

Isaiah 46:9-13 (KJV)

The word **_declaring_** found in Isaiah 46:9 is from the Hebrew word:

נָגַד nāgad <u><H5046></u>—a primitive root; properly to *front*, i.e. stand boldly out opposite; by implication (causative), **_to manifest; figurative to announce (always by word of mouth to one present); specifically to expose, predict, explain, praise_** :- certify, declare (-ing), expound fully, a messenger, plainly, profess, rehearse, report, show (forth), speak, tell, utter.

—Strong's Concordance

The word declaring is showing us that Yahweh is making known the end of his plan from the beginning. This is a wonderful secret that I will make known in this work how Yahweh is shown to have declared the end from the beginning. This involves ancient history that has been deliberately removed from the minds of mankind. This involved a process he allowed for the purpose of proving what he had warned certain beings in heaven from, who were determined to prove him wrong. These beings were taught if they violate the universal laws of peace they would bring upon themselves death and destruction. The beginning the prophet Isaiah is speaking of must be understood by the reader, because it is describing a time prior to Adam. The Holy Scripture describes two beginnings one that preceded Adam and Eve, and the recreation of both the heavens and the earth. This is also an ancient history describing destruction, and its effect on both the heavens and the earth. The Holy Scripture describes these events as the genealogical history of both the heavens and the earth. Notice this in the following scriptures:

These *are* the generations of the heavens and of the earth when they were created, in the day that Yahweh made the earth and the heavens.

Gen 2:4 (KJV)

Written by
Yibniyah Hawkins
5/27/2013

The word **"generations"** written in Genesis 2:4 is from the Hebrew word:

תּוֹלְדֹת tôlēdôt <H8435>—or *toledah*, to-led-aw'; from <H3205> (yalad); (plural only) *descent*, i.e. *family*; *(figurative) history: - birth, generations*.

—Strong's Concordance

תּוֹלְדֹת tôlēdôt : is also found in the Gesenius's Hebrew Lexicon by Samuel page 859 shows this word to mean:

תּוֹלְדֹת f. pl. (from the root יָלַד)—(1) *generations, families, races*, Nu. 1:20, seqq. לְתוֹלְדֹתָם according to their races, Gen. 10:32; 25:13; Exod. 6:16. Hence סֵפֶר תּוֹלְדֹת *genealogy, pedigree*, Gen. 5:1. As a very large portion of the most ancient Oriental history consists of genealogies, it means—

(2) *history*, properly of families. Gen. 6:9, אֵלֶּה תּוֹלְדֹת נֹחַ "this is the history of Noah." Genesis 37:2; and thus also applied to the *origin* of other things. Gen. 2:4, " this is the origin of the heaven and earth." (Compare יַחַשׂ and Syr. ܟܬ݂ܒ family, genealogy, history.)

The word generation means the genealogical history which consisted of the genealogies given to us in the book of Genesis. The names given to us in the genealogy of the patriarchs of old reveal ancient history concerning both the heavens and the earth. This history was recorded in this manner through an ancient art describe for us in a work entitle "The Hebraic Tongue Restored by Fabre de Olivet. Dr. Olivet describes the use of proper names composed artfully to hide

Written by
Yibniyah Hawkins
5/27/2013

details concerning events, and knowledge concerning the creation of the heavens and the earth. Notice this on page 122, 173 in the Hebraic Tongue Restored:

v. 1. אֶת־קַיִן, *the-self-sameness of-Kain*.... Need I speak of the importance that the peoples of the Orient have attached to proper names, and of what deep mysteries their sages have often hidden beneath these names? Had I space here to express myself in this subject, my only perplexity would be making a choice among the numberless proofs. But the time is short and these notes are already too voluminous. The intellectual reader has no need of a vain display of useless erudition, to be taught what he already knows. Let it suffice therefore, for me to say that Moses is the one, of the writers of antiquity, who has developed most subtly the art of composing proper names. I have endeavoured to give an idea of his talent, or that of his instructors in this respect, by developing the name of universal man אָדָם, *collective unity, eternal similitude*, and that of the Supreme Divinity יְהוֹה, *the Being who is, who was, and who will be*. But I must make it clear that these two names, and some others, were sufficiently elevated by their nature to be translatable without danger. The names which follow will be, almost all, a very different matter. Moses has been often obliged to throw over them a veil, that I ought and wish to respect. Although I might perhaps give the literal word, I shall not do so. I inform my reader of this in order that he may be watchful: for if he desire it, nothing shall prevent him from knowing.

One ought not to forget besides, what I have said pertaining to the extreme importance that the ancients attach to *proper names*; it cannot be given too great attention. Notwithstanding the length of my notes and even the numerous repetitions into which I purposely fall, it will always be well for the reader to consult the Radical Vocabulary for the signification of their roots.

There is Nothing New Under the Sun

The history concerning the creation of the heavens and the earth are hidden in a unique manner in the first 10 chapters of Genesis. The history I want to focus on today is described as the first beginning, a time known in scripture as an ancient time. This is a time when Yahweh proved through his infinite wisdom what he had warned the heavenly kingdoms against. In a time described in scripture as an ancient time there arouses many heavenly begins who had determined to rebel against Yahweh and his righteous kingdom. They began to doubt Yahweh who was admonishing them to remain true to the way of life he created for all creation to exist in. He also taught them the curses that would develop when one breaks the laws he taught and explain in detail to this heavenly host. There was no evidence document to prove what Yahweh was strongly admonishing them to refrain from. This lead to an increasing degree of skepticism and disbelief in the curses Yahweh was warning them against. This also lead to a counsel of heavenly begins who decided to undertake a life of sin. This history is describe briefly in book of Psalm were Yahweh is described as standing (judging) in the mist of an assembly. Notice this in the following scriptures

Yahweh stands in the congregation of the mighty; he judges among the gods. How long will you judge unjustly, and accept the persons of the wicked? Selah. **You should** defend the poor and fatherless: do justice to the afflicted and needy. Deliver the poor and needy: rid *them* out of the hand of the wicked. You know not, neither will they understand; they walk on in darkness: all the foundations of the earth are out of course because of you. I have said, you *are* gods; and all of you *are* children of the most high. But you shall die like men, and fall like one of the princes.

Psalms 82:1-7 (KJV)

In this scripture Yahweh is addressing an assembly who he said would "die like mankind" and fall like rulers on earth". Surely these are begins who once lived and were taught the ways of righteousness, but they choose to rebel and undertake a

Written by
Yibniyah Hawkins
5/27/2013

life of sin. Notice the phrase in the above scripture which says *__all the foundation of the earth are out of course because of you__*. The ancient history_that we will divulge into describes in detail the foundations of the earth which includes all the life given function of both heaven and earth, its rotation, the proper amount of sun light and the atmosphere we depend on for life was completely destroyed in the beginning. It was in this time the scripture describes three undertakings which were similar to Lucifer's Rebellion. There were three other beings who have attempted to created a new reality (new world order) were a "Great Undertaking" would be realized. This undertaking was to prove that one could live forever without following Yahweh's 613 Laws of righteousness, but instead indulge in sin without experience the curses Yahweh had warn them about. All three of these undertaking ended with destruction which spread throughout the universe. This was known from the beginning as the "great experiment" we will explain fully this in the preceding chapters in this work. It is from this experiment that Yahweh collected enough evidence to prove that his way is right and from this he was able to declare the end from the beginning. It was his righteous laws that they rejected in each one these undertakings, which proved his laws were right, and would lead all nations into peace. The prophet Isaiah was inspired to write that an anointed one of two witnesses would reveal to the world the former things. Notice this in the following scriptures.

Let all the nations be gathered together, and let the people be assembled: who among them can declare this, **and show us former things**? Let them bring forth their witnesses, that they may be justified: or let them hear, and say, *it is* truth. You *are* my witnesses, says Yahweh, and my servant whom I have chosen: that you may know and believe me, and understand that I *am* he: before me there was no God formed, neither shall there be after me. I, *even* I, *am* Yahweh; and beside me *there is* no savior. I have declared, and have saved, and I have showed, when *there was* no strange *god* among you: therefore ye *are* my witnesses, says Yahweh, that I *am* Yahweh.

Isaiah 43:9-12 (KJV)

Written by
Yibniyah Hawkins
5/27/2013

There is Nothing New Under the Sun

I have not spoken in secret, in a dark place of the earth: I did not say to the seed of Jacob, Seek ye me in vain: I Yahweh speak righteousness; I declare things that are right. Assemble yourselves and come; draw near together, ye *that are* escaped of the nations: they have no knowledge that set up the wood of their graven image, and pray unto a god *that* cannot save. Tell you, and bring *your proof* near; yes, let them take counsel together: ___who has declared this from ancient time? Who has declared it from that time? Have not I Yahweh? And there is no Source of power beside me; a just Father and a Saviour; there is none beside me___. Look to me, and be saved, all the ends of the earth: for I *am* Yahweh, and *there is* none else.

Isaiah 45:19-22 (KJV)

__Remember the former things of old__: for I *am* Yahweh, and *there is* none else; *I am* Yahweh, and *there is* none like me, ___Declaring the end from the beginning, and from ancient times the things that are not yet done, saying, My counsel shall stand, and I will do all my plan___: Calling an eagle from the east, the man that executes my counsel from a far country: yea, I have spoken *it*, I will also bring it to pass; I have purposed *it*, I will also do it.

Isaiah 46:9-11 (KJV)

I beg the reader to remember what I am presenting as an introduction to the chapters that will follow. This is a great secret Isaiah the prophet was inspired to write for us, it is from this time Yahweh declared the end of his plan of salvation from events occurring in ancient times. These are the former things He is calling the nations to consider, and for the two witness to proclaim to the entire world. Notice in Isaiah 46:10 the phrase ___"and from ancient times things that are not yet done"___ This should give the reader a clue to what is hidden hear concerning the events that transpired in a time prior to the renovation of the earth for the placing of Adam and Eve in the Garden of Eden. The second beginning which included the plan to allow 7,000 years of history to unfold here on earth which allows mankind to go there own way. In this history he has allotted mankind a 6,000 year time period. In this time period their technological advancement will increase given them the capability to destroy the earth just as they did in ancient times. Yahweh

Written by
Yibniyah Hawkins
5/27/2013

has now called both heaven and earth to witness 7,000 years of history which he declared all things that will occur until the end of this 7,000 year period from the beginning. The nations must consider this history seriously because it shows us the love Yahweh has for all creation, and his desire to guide all nations and people alike from destroying themselves, and the earth which he created for mankind.

Chapter Two

Considering the Former Things

The former things spoken of in the Holy Scripture is an ancient history Yahweh has commanded to be declared to nations. This history corresponds to the time period we are in, and it was from this ancient time Yahweh was able to predict the end from the beginning. The prophet Isaiah was inspired to write concerning the former days and the commission of two witnesses to cause all nations to consider the former days. Notice this in the following scriptures:

Let all the nations be gathered together, and let the people be assembled: who among them can declare this, *__and show us former things__*? *__Let them bring forth their witnesses, that they may be justified: or let them hear, and say, it is truth__*.

Isaiah 43:9 (KJV)

Notice the phrase in the above scripture "*who among them can declare this, and show us former things?*" It is important we declared this to the nations, because the former things or events, that transpired on this earth are to deter the nation from bring on themselves destruction. The two witnesses are given the command from Yahweh as we will see to cause the nation to consider the former events we can now prove took place here on earth. The word **former** is defined in the Webster Dictionary with this meaning:

Former: Webster Dictionary page 752: Preceding in time; a prior or earlier time; Long past and ancient 3. Preceding in order; being the first of two; being also the first mention of two earlier periods or ages.

The word former is describing an ancient time or ages were events were allowed to transpire here on earth for the purpose of saving all creation. The events of this time are to be remembered and recount to mankind. They were to prove to man that to undertake a life of sin with hopes of peace is impossible, and Yahweh proved this in a time called in scripture the beginning. _In this time was a catastrophic planet-wide destruction that change the surface of the earth, decimated human and animal life, changed its climate, push up mountains and submerge the whole earth under water_. This destruction is described in detail in the Holy Scripture as former events that Yahweh commanded to be remembered. We will reveal the violent modification of the earth's climate and the orbit of the planets which cause destruction to spread throughout the Milky Way. There were powers developed in this time period that resembles the nuclear bomb we have today. _**"Is it possible that nuclear war and destructive climate disturbance occurred here on earth prior to placing of Adam and Eve in the garden?"**_ The answer to this question is yes! We will reveal this both from scripture and secular history that has been recorded for us. The former things inspired to be written for us is what the prophet Isaiah is inspiring to be declared and considered by the nations. Notice this in the following scriptures.

Present your cause, says Yahweh; bring forth your strong _reasons_, says the King of Jacob. Let them bring _them_ forth, and show us what shall happen: _**"let them show the former things, what they be, that we may consider them, and know the latter**_

Written by
Yibniyah Hawkins
5/27/2013

There is Nothing New Under the Sun

end of them; or declare us things to come." Show the things that are to come hereafter, that we may know that ye *are* gods: yea, do good, or do evil, that we may be dismayed, and behold *it* together. Behold, you *are* nothing, and your work of nothing: an abomination *is he that* chooses you. I have raised up *one* from the north, and he shall come: from the rising of the sun shall he call upon my name: and he shall come upon princes as *upon* mortar, and as the potter treaded clay.
Who has declared from the beginning, that we may know? And former times, that we may say, He is righteous? Yes, there is none that shows, yes, there is none that declares, yes, there is none that hears your words.

Isaiah 41:21-26 (KJV)

I have declared the former things from the beginning; and they went forth out of my mouth, and I made them known; I did them suddenly, and they came to pass.
Because I knew that you *were* obstinate, and your neck *is* an iron sinew, and your brow brass; *I have even from the beginning declared it to you; before it came to pass I revealed it you: so you could not say, Mine idol(God) has done them, nor my graven image, and my molten image, has commanded them. You have heard, and seen all of this; will you not declare it? I have showed you new things from this time, even hidden things, and you did not know them.* They are created now, and not from the beginning. Have not heard of them before this day.so you cannot say, Behold, I knew them.

Isaiah 48:3-7 (KJV)

The prophet Isaiah shows Yahweh declared the former things from the beginning, and he expounds on this by revealing to us an event that occurred in an ancient time period. Notice this in the following scriptures

Awake, awake, put on strength, O arm of Yahweh; awake, *as in the ancient days, in the generations of old*. *Was it* not you who *cut Rahab, and wounded the dragon? Was it not you who* *dried the sea, the waters of the great deep*; Who made the depths of the sea a way for the ransomed to pass over?

Isaiah 51:9-10 (KJV)

Written by
Yibniyah Hawkins
5/27/2013

There is Nothing New Under the Sun

The word **ancient** written in Isaiah 51:9 is from the Hebrew word:

קֶדֶם qedem <u><H6924></u>—**qedmah**, kayd'-maw; from <u><H6923></u> (qadam); the *front*, of place (absolute the *fore part*, relative the *East*) or *time (antiquity)*; **often used adverbially (before, anciently, eastward)**:- aforetime, ancient (time), before, old, past. Compare <u><H6926></u> (qidmah).

Notice the word ***antiquity*** define in the Hebrew word "qedem" is found in the Webster Dictionary page 93

Antiquity: An ancient time or former ages; belonging to the past and not modern; dating from a period long ago.

The word ancient times is revealing to us a time long ago that preceded the placing of Adam and Eve in the Garden of Eden. In this time plans were made to allow the destruction documented for us in biblical history to take place as a preventive occurrence to stop the progression of the curse's that could destroy both heaven and earth. Notice the word **generation** written in Isaiah 51: 9 is from the Hebrew word:

דּוֹר dôr <u><H1755></u>—**dor**, dore; from <u><H1752></u> (duwr); properly a *revolution* of time, i.e. ***an age or generation***; also a *dwelling* :- age—Strong's Concordance

The Hebrew word דּוֹר dôr is also found in the Hebraic Tongue Restored by Fabre de Olivet page 325 -326 with this meaning.

דּר **DR.** This root, composed of the sign of abund-ance born of division, united to the elementary root אר, characterizes the temporal state of things, the age, cycle,

Written by
Yibniyah Hawkins
5/27/2013

order, generation, time. Thence רד, every idea of cycle, period, life, customs, epoch, generation, abode.

דור   Action of *ordering* a thing, *disposing* of it following a certain order; *resting* in any sphere whatsoever; *dwelling* in a place; *living* in an age: that which *circulates*, that which *exists* according to a movement and a regulated order. *An orb, universe, world, circuit; a city.*

דרר   (*intens.*)   The broad and generalized idea of circulating without obstacle, of following a natural movement, brings forth the idea of *liberty*, the state of *being free*, the action of *acting without constraint*.

The word generation is defined as ancient ages were two orders "systems of government" were in existence. In this time period if you would notice from the definition of the Hebrew word "dor" is describing a time distinguish by a particular event and a state of affairs that caused destruction in both the heavens and the earth. The system of government in existence at that time was striving to put an end to the destruction and curses brought forth by an evil system of government describe by Isaiah as Rahab and the dragon. The system of government in existence in the beginning striving against kingdom of darkness was known from the beginning as the Order of Melchizedek. This system of government was a Government of Peace and Government of Righteousness striving to establish lasting peace and justice throughout the entire universe. The Government of Peace that Melechizedek came to represent is the eternal kingdom of Yahweh that many heavenly beings undertook to overthrow and rebel against. The revealing of who Melechizedek was will not be expounded on in this work but I admonish the reader to acquire our work entitle "Babylon an Apostate City".

Let's return to Isaiah 51:9 and let's learn more about this system of government described to use by the prophet Isaiah.

Written by
Yibniyah Hawkins
5/27/2013

There is Nothing New Under the Sun

Notice first the word **cut** written in Isaiah 51:9 is from the Hebrew word

 Awake, awake, put on strength, O arm of Yahweh; awake, as in the ancient days, in the generations of old. *Was it not You who **cut Rahab, and wounded the dragon?***

Isaiah 51:9 (KJV)

חָצֵב ḥāṣēb <H2672>— when the word "haseb" is reduced to it primitive root is from the Hebrew word חֵץ ḥēṣ <H2671— from <H2686> (chatsats); properly **_a piercer, i.e. an arrow; by implication a wound; figurative (of God) thunder-bolt_**; (by interchange for <H6086> (`ets)) the *shaft* of a spear :- + archer, arrow, dart, shaft, staff, wound.

— Strong's Concordance

The word ***"cut"*** is describing a weapon called the ***"thunder-bolt of the gods"***. Please remember this name, because as we proceed in this work you will see history preserved on earth that called and describes a destructive weapon by this name. This weapon caused great destruction and alteration in the atmosphere of the earth in the beginning. Notice the name of the system of government that caused destruction in the earth and its self destroyed as a result. Notice the name ***"Rahab"*** written in Isaiah 51:9 is from the Hebrew word:

רַהַב rahab <H7294>—the same as <H7293> (rahab); *Rahab* (i.e. *boaster*), an epithet of Egypt: - Rahab—Strong's Concordance

רָהַב rāhab <H7292—a primitive root; to *urge* severely, i.e. (figurative) *importune, embolden, capture, and act insolently*: - overcome, behave self proudly, make sure, strengthen.

Strong's Concordance

רָהַב rāhab— is defined in the Hebrew and English Lexicon by Brown-Driver& Briggs page 923: Is describe as a sea monster because of its character: to act stormily, boisterously, arrogantly; To storm against; an emblematic name of a mystical sea monster who is describe as having boisterous and raging behavior.

רָהַב rāhab: is defined in the Hebrew and Chaldee Lexicon to Old Testament by Julius Furst page 1283 with following meaning.: To rage, to be furious; to bustle or to terrify, to put into alarm or fear. 2_. Egypt itself receives the name of Rahab in later books, typifying a tumultuous violence._

In Hebrew the use of proper names were used to disclose details concerning events in a given time period hidden in the names given by the prophets. The name Rahab is used here to describe not only a system of government in existence in an ancient time, but also the events centered on its existence. When the name Rahab used to describe this ancient nation is examined under an ancient code called **"permutation"** the name Rahab reveals some incredible information. This code is based on a unique etymological root system used in the art of writing in days of old. The code brings forth a **_"secret formula"_** were it uses a set number of Hebrew consonants, that are applied to a word by special grammatical rules. The formula brings forth a special combination of etymological roots revealing knowledge, wisdom, and detail events concerning past, present and future prophecies. I will not exhaust the reader with all the methods used to acquire the information revealed by this code, but I will make known the meaning of the etymological root words revealed by the code.

The name Rahab used by the prophet Isaiah is revealing to us the nature and character of this nation who is describe as sea monster because of its character. The Hebrew word describes Rahab as a very distinct nation in a particular region of the earth who is describe as acting boisterously, arrogantly ruling with violence, and serving as the cause of trouble and calamity amongst the inhabitants of the earth. They assumed preeminence over others despising, humiliating, and scorning them in their arrogant pride. They deprive others of their rights, their property, and freedom because of their great military might. The name Rahab describing this nation reveals the iniquity and injustice that establish them as superior nation at that time. Notice the etymological roots establish by the art of permutations applied to the Hebrew word "רָהַב rāhab"

Written by
Yibniyah Hawkins
5/27/2013

מר   **MR.**   The sign of exterior and passive action being united to that of movement proper, constitutes a root whose purpose is to characterize that which gives way to its impulsion, which extends itself, usurps or invades space; but when this same sign is linked by contraction to the root אר symbol of elementary principle, then the root which results is applied to all the modifications of this same element.

The Arabic مر contained primitively the same ideas as the Hebraic root.   In the modern idiom this root is limited to two principal acceptations; the first is applied to the action of *passing, exceeding, going beyond;* the second, to the state of being bitter, strong, sturdy.

מר   That which extending and rising, affects *the empire, the dominion;* as a *potentate*: that which exceeds the limits of one's authority; as *a tyrant, a rebel*: that which is attached to the idea of elementary principle, as *an atom.*

The are many things this root reveals to us concerning this nation first notice the nation is described as being given up to a impulsion, that is an impelling force (influence) , that compels and persuades this nation to sin. The sin described in this word is "one going beyond and exceeding the limit's of their authority, by modifying the elementary principle the **_"atom"_**. This modification of the *"atom"* is iniquity (a deviation from a prescribe function), and a perversion (a turning from the proper use) the elementary principle "the atom". This word is describing a deviation from the ordinances of heaven and earth that Yahweh establishes in his laws. The ordinances of heaven and earth established two reactions we find in

Written by
Yibniyah Hawkins
5/27/2013

creation the fission and fusion reaction. The fusion reaction creates life and light a process necessary for all life. Through a fusion process called the "helium process" the helium atoms come together to form carbon the life giving element. The fusion reaction is the process of putting matter together and the fission reaction is process of forcefully splitting apart of matter. The fission process is "illegal" according to the ordinances of Yahweh for both heaven and earth ***"when its process is altered from its proper usage establish by Yahweh"***. The nuclear fission of atoms by the use of fissionable material (*like the atoms of uranium*) which converts part of the mass into energy can be used as a weapon of war. The fission process can create a bomb whose explosive force can destroy both heaven and earth.

The Hebrew word Rahab is describing in detail what we establish earlier in the word *"cut"* which describes a weapon similar to a arrow called the "**thunderbolt of the gods**" which caused destruction to both the earth and the atmosphere. Notice the unique root words found in the name Rahab describing the effect of a weapon which alters the use of the atom, resulting in the destruction of an ancient nation. Notice this from the Hebraic Tongue Restored by Fabre de'Olivet pages 307,338, 297

בֹּעַ **BHO.** Every idea of precipitate, harsh, inordinate movement. It is the root בֹּא, in which the mother vowel has degenerated toward the material sense.

בָּעָה *An anxious inquiry, a search; a turgescence, a boiling; action of boiling, etc.*

The Arabic بَاعَ signifies in a restricted sense, *to sell* and *to buy*, to make a negotiation; بَعَ *to interfere* for another, and *to prompt* him in what he should say. The word بَاعَ which springs from the primitive root בֹּעַ, contains all ideas of iniquity and of injustice.

Written by
Yibniyah Hawkins
5/27/2013

וָר   OUR. Onomatopoetic root which depicting the noise of the air and the wind, denotes figuratively, that which *is fanned, puffed with wind, vain.* In Arabic و,ر.

The verb ورر which appears to be attached to the root אר, characterizes the state of that which is sharp, which cleaves the air with rapidity.

נא   ZA. Every idea of movement and of direction; noise, the terror which results therefrom: *a dart; a luminous ray; an arrow, a flash.*

The Arabic زازا indicates, as onomatopoetic root the state of being shaken in the air, the noise made by the thing shaken.

בער   (*comp.*) Every idea of *devastation* by fire, *annihilation, conflagration, combustion, consuming heat:* that which *destroys, ravages;* that which makes *desert and arid,* speaking of the earth; *brutish* and *stupid,* speaking of men. It is the root עַר, governed by the sign of interior activity ב.

אף **APH.** **Sign of power united to that of speech,** constitutes a root, which characterizes in a broad sense, that which leads to a goal, to any end whatsoever; *a final cause.* Hieroglyphically, this root was symbolized by the image of a *wheel.* Figuratively, one deduced all ideas of impulse, transport, envelopment in a sort of vortex, etc.

The Arabic ﺍﻑ is an onomatopoetic root, developing all ideas of disgust, ennui, indignation. In the ancient language it was received in the same sense as the Hebrew

The above root words derive from the Hebrew word Rahab describes actions and activities which exceeded the proper and reasonable limits for peace, causing iniquity and injustice to abound within the earth. The roots describes a weapon which is similar to an arrow or luminous ray which is shaken (exploded in the air) causing devastation and annihilation by fire. This brought about a consuming heat that destroyed and ravaged the earth causing atmospheric disturbance which produced droughts, hurricanes and floods. This will be expounded on further in the coming chapters. Let's return to Isayah 51:9

Awake, awake, put on strength, O arm of Yahweh! Awake, as in the ancient days, in the generations of old. *Was it not you who have* cut Rahab, *and **wounded the dragon?***

Isaiah 51:9 (KJV)

Notice the word ***wounded*** *written in Isaiah 51:9 is from the Hebrew word:*

חָלַל *ḥālal* <u><H2490</u> which means: to *pierced* (especially to death); figurative *polluted*: - kill, profane, slain, × slew, (deadly) wounded. —Strong's Concordance

This word wounded is revealing the destroying and slaying of the dragon. The question might be what is the dragon here spoken of by Isayah the prophet?

Written by
Yibniyah Hawkins
5/27/2013

The word dragon written in Isayah 51:9 is from the Hebrew word:

תַּנִּין tannîn <H8577>— *tanniym*, tan-neem'; (Ezek. 29:3), intensive from the same as <H8565> (tan); a marine or land *monster*, i.e. *sea-serpent* or *jackal*: - dragon, sea-monster, serpent, whale.

Strong's Concordance

תַּנִּין tannîn <H8577> is also found in the Hebrew Chaldee Lexicon to Old Testament by Julius Fuerst page 1483: A sea- monster Job 7:12 a figure of dangerous enemy, and a symbol of the all devouring Babylonian Empire and consequently equivalent to "לִוְיָתָן" (leviathan). Notice the meaning of the Hebrew word:

לִוְיָתָן liwyātān <H3882 in the Hebrew and Chaldee Lexicon by Juliuis Fuerst page 737-738:

1. A Serpent (Isaiah 27:1) 2. Metaphorically: the dragon in heaven Job 3:8 Job 26:13: a constellation which follows the sun and the moon according to Eastern myth, *sometimes surrounds them and so brings on darkness,* a thing which magicians also were said to be able to accomplish.; *Great powers were symbolized as strong animals and represented as sea-monsters (Daniel 7:3).*

The word dragon is also found in the Hebraic Tongue Restored page: 315-316:

جّ That which *encloses, surrounds* or *covers* all parts; that which forms *the enclosure* of a thing; *limits* this thing and *protects it;* in the same fashion that a sheath encloses, limits and protects its blade.

The Arabic جْن has all the acceptations of the Hebraic root. It is, in general, everything which covers or which surrounds another; it is, in particular, a protecting *shade, a darkness,* as much physically as morally; *a tomb.* As verb, this word expresses the action of enveloping with darkness, making night, obscuring the mind, rendering foolish, covering with a veil, enclosing with walls, etc. In

the ancient idiom جِن has signified *a demon, a devil, a dragon;* جنان *a shield;* جنون *bewilderment* of mind; جنين

The word dragon is revealing to us the motivating force behind the iniquity we see leading Rahab to destroy themselves and the earth. This word dragon is speaking of the rule of darkness which caused the minds of these begins to be obscured void of Light (the laws of righteousness). The dragon is symbolic of the spirit of darkness which is indentified with the demonic forces of the earth leading mankind to cause the earth to become a desolated waste place. The dragon represents the dark forces of the earth causing misery, death, destruction, falsehood, deception and wickedness to abound on earth. Yahweh is shown here to have deadly wounded this dragon (the rule of darkness) by permitting them to destroy not only themselves but also the earth. There have been many scholars who have associated Isaiah 51:9-10 with Exodus and the parting of the Red Sea, but this scripture is declaring events that occurred long before the parting of the Red Sea. Notices with me in verse 10 were Isaiah gives the key to this event being established in ancient time.

Written by
Yibniyah Hawkins
5/27/2013

There is Nothing New Under the Sun

Was it not you who have dried the sea, the waters of the great deep; who made the depths of the sea a way for the ransomed to pass over?

Isaiah 51:10 (KJV)

In the Exodus Yahweh is shown to have divided the sea, but Isaiah shows he dried the sea in an ancient time. Notice this in the following scriptures:

And Moses stretched out his hand over the sea; and Yahweh caused the sea to go *back* by a strong east wind all that night, and made the sea dry *land*, and the waters were divided. And the children of Israel went into the midst of the sea upon the dry *ground*: and the waters *were* a wall unto them on their right hand, and on their left.

Ex 14:21-22 (KJV)

Isayah is inspired to write in Isaiah 51:10 that Yahweh *"dried"* the sea, the waters of the great deep! Notice with me the word *"dried"* written Isaiah 51:10 is from the Hebrew word:

חָרֵב ḥārēb <H2717— or ***chareb***, khaw-rabe'; a primitive root; to *parch* (through drought), i.e. (by analogy) to *desolate,* (be) desolate, (be) dry (up), (lay, lie, make) waste. Drought also was used as cutting instrument from its destructive effects; implement that can be used in war.

—Strong's Concordance

חָרֵב ḥārēb: is found in Genenius Hebrew and Chaldee Lexicon page 301-302:

חָרַב whence imp. חֲרֹב, and חָרֵב future יֶחֱרַב—
(1) TO BE DRIED UP, spoken of water, rivers, earth. Gen. 8:13; Job 14:11; Isai. 19:6; Ps. 106:9. It differs ["as merely denoting the absence of water"] from יָבֵשׁ *to be dry, to become dried,* see Gen. 8:13,

Written by
Yibniyah Hawkins
5/27/2013

חֹרֶב m.—(1) *dryness, drought,* Jud. 6:37-39; hence, *heat,* Gen. 31:40; Job 30:30.

Notice this is speaking of a drought which is also used by Yahweh as an instrument of correction and deliverance. Notice the rest of verse 10 which says he caused the waters of the great deep to be dried up by drought. The word **"deep"** written in Isayah 51:10 is from the Hebrew word:

תְּהוֹם tehôm <H8415— or *tehom*, teh-home'; (usually feminine) from <H1949> (huwm); an *abyss* (as a *surging* mass of water), especially the *deep* (the *main* sea or the subterranean *water-supply*) Tehom means: deep water; ocean; flood of waters; It used of the ocean in contrast to the sea— The New Strong's Expanded Exhaustive Concordance of the Bible Red Letter Edition.

The phrase great deep is not speaking of a sea but an ocean like the Atlantic Ocean which in this time Yahweh caused it to become dried up. We will reveal the detail of this event because it is recorded again for us in the Holy Scripture in great detail. There may be some who are saying; who is the ransomed who pass over? I will reiterate again for those who would like to research this Isaiah is speaking of an ancient time and not the time of Mosheh. I will not expound on this point in this work, but in a future work we will reveal who this ransomed who pass over was! Notice with me in he following scripture in Isaiah 51 were the prophet himself shows a distinction between the two events. I beg the reader to read all of Isaiah 51 because in it you will find Isaiah comforting the righteous, that Yahweh will deliver them from the oppressor and the kingdom of darkness. He comforts them by recounted to them an ancient time when Yahweh destroyed the kingdom of darkness and another time when he delivered them from Egypt. Egypt who in a later time period was described by the prophets to resemble Rahab a very proud and ruthless nation. Notice this fact in the following scripture were the prophet shows a distinction between the two events.

Written by
Yibniyah Hawkins
5/27/2013

There is Nothing New Under the Sun

Therefore the redeemed of Yahweh shall return, and come with singing unto Zion; and everlasting joy *shall be* upon their head: they shall obtain gladness and joy; *and* sorrow and mourning shall flee away. I, *even* I, *am* he that comforts you: who *art* you, that you should be afraid of a man *that* shall die, and of the son of man *which* shall be made *as* grass; And forget Yahweh your maker, that has stretched forth the heavens, and laid the foundations of the earth; You have feared continually every day because of the fury of the oppressor, as if he were ready to destroy? And where *is* the fury of the oppressor? The captive exile hastens that he may be loosed, and that he should not die in the pit, nor that his bread should fail. ***But I am Yahweh your Father who divided the sea, whose waves roared: Yahweh of hosts is his name.***

Isaiah 51:11-15 (KJV)

I introduce this event of the cutting of Rahab and wounding of the dragon to reveal the former things Yahweh wants all nations to consider. We will go even deeper into this subject, because the two witnesses are commanded to cause all nations to consider these former events. Yahweh who allowed these events to take place on earth did so for a purpose. We will reveal the purpose for Yahweh allowing these events, which included the use of a weapon which is similar to the atomic and nuclear arsenal we have today. This weapon caused both the heavens and the earth to be destroyed is recorded for us in the Holy Scripture. Yahweh wants all nations to consider the former things so they can avoid the destruction he alone knows will occur. Notice this in the following scriptures were Yahweh calls all nation to present there case!

Present your cause, says Yahweh; bring forth your strong *reasons*, says the King of Jacob. Let them bring *them* forth, and show us what shall take place***: let them show the former things, what they were, so we may consider them, and know the latter end of them; or declare to us things to come.*** *Show the things that are to come hereafter, that we may know that ye are gods: yes, do good, or do evil, that we may be dismayed, and behold it together. Behold, you are of nothing, and your work of nothing: an abomination is he that choose you.* Who has declared from the beginning, that we may know? And former times, that we may say, *He is*

Written by
Yibniyah Hawkins
5/27/2013

righteous? Yes, *there is* none that shows, yes, *there is* none that declares, yes, *there is* none that hears your words.

Isaiah 41:21-26 (KJV)

Let all the nations be gathered together, and let the people be assembled: who among them can declare this, **_and show us former things?_** Let them bring forth their witnesses, that they may be justified: or let them hear, and say, *it is* truth.

Isaiah 43:9 (KJV)

Remember the former things of old: for I *am* Yahweh, and *there is* none else; *I am* Yahweh, and *there is* none like me

Isaiah 46:9 (KJV)

Yahweh is pleading with all nations to consider the former things(events) because it was by these events being allowed to take place here on earth, that Yahweh is able to" Declare the end from the beginning." In the above scripture Isaiah 46:9 Yahweh commands us to remember the former things. He also inspired Isayah to write there is none like him who can declare the end from the beginning! Notice this fact in the following scriptures

Remember the former things of old: for I *am* Yahweh, and *there is* none else; *I am* Yahweh, and *there is* none like me, **_Declaring the end from the beginning, and from ancient times the things that are not yet done, saying, My counsel shall stand, and I will fulfill all My plan:_**

Isaiah 46:9-10 (KJV)

I have not spoken in secret, in a dark place of the earth: I said not unto the seed of Jacob, Seek me in vain: **_I Yahweh speak righteousness; I declare things that are right._** Assemble yourselves and come; draw near together, you *that are* escaped of the nations: they have no knowledge that set up the wood of their graven image, and pray unto a god *that* cannot save. Speak out, and bring *them* near; yes, let them

Written by
Yibniyah Hawkins
5/27/2013

take counsel together: ***Who has declared this from ancient time? Who has told it from that time? Have not I Yahweh? And there is no sources of power expect me; a just Father and a Saviour; there is none beside me. Look unto me, and be saved, all the ends of the earth: for I am Yahweh, and there is none else.***

Isaiah 45:19-22 (KJV)

Let explore how Yahweh is able to declare the end from the beginning, because it is the events recorded for us in the beginning, that we will be able to convince the governments of man to destroy all weapons of war.

Chapter Three

An Ancient History of the Heavens and the Earth

In the Beginnings

In the first three verse of Genesis chapter one is the preamble of the Government of Yahweh revealed to all the inhabitants of the earth. A preamble is an introductory statement, a preface which states the reason and the intent of something. A preamble is also described as a "preliminary or introductory fact" concerning specific circumstances needing to be resolved. The first three verse of Genesis reveals an ancient history which includes a plan to stop sin, and the curses sin brings from destroying all creation. The introductory statement brings to light an ancient history concerning the destruction of both the heavens and the earth. Let's define the word preamble for the sake of clarity.

Preamble: is found in the Webster Dictionary with this meaning: *A statement introductory to and explanatory of what follows; the introductory portion of a writing used chiefly of formal resolutions. (L. praeambulum origin from praeambulus which means "walking before" Syn: beginning, prologue, prelude and a foreword.*

The first three verses of Genesis are written as a preamble which introduces us to a plan to stop sin and death. It describes Yahweh as **"walking before"** that is witnessing and permitting the events describe in the first three verse of Genesis. The preamble includes resolutions to solve the issues which are causing a degree of uncertainty in the universe. There were beings in heaven who doubted Yahweh and his righteous laws. They had prior to their "Undertaking to sin" experience none of the curses Yahweh had emphatically warned them against. Yahweh like Yahshua the firstborn of the sons of men did not need to experience sin to believe what He had through his wisdom wrote in the form of laws to guide all creation away from death. The laws of Yahweh establishes a way of life that leads one from all death, that is anything a person could do or practice that would eventually cause him to die. An example of this are the laws of Yahweh which says you should not fornicate, commit adultery or covet what belongs to your brother. When these laws are broken they bring death to the human body in the form of debilitating diseases or death by wars. These heavenly begins would not guide there lives by the wisdom embedded in Yahweh's law which reveals the curses one bring into his life when these laws are violated. They begin to doubt Yahweh and his righteous laws and undertook away of life to prove him wrong, this eventually led to violent wars, and devastating diseases throughout his government. The first three verse of Genesis introduce one to the events that transpired in both the heavens and the

Written by
Yibniyah Hawkins
5/27/2013

earth. The Government of Peace (also known has the Kingdom of Yahweh) formed a plan to stop this undertaking to sin, and this plan begins with a preliminary account of events, that transpire in both the heaven and the earth. The Plan of Yahweh starts with the introductory statement "In the beginning" which goes on to explain specific events that came to pass in an ancient time. The reader will learn from this chapter details concerning the events Yahweh permitted for a purpose. Let's begin are study in Genesis 1: 1-5

 In the beginning Yahweh created the heaven and the earth. ***And the earth was without form, and void; and darkness was upon the face of the deep.*** And the Spirit of Yahweh moved upon the face of the waters.

 And Yahweh said, Let there be light: and there was light. And Yahweh saw the light, that *it was* good: and Yahweh divided the light from the darkness. And Yahweh called the light Day, and the darkness he called Night. And the evening and the morning were the first day.

Gen 1:1-5 (KJV)

The word ***in*** written in Genesis 1:1 is from the Hebrew preposition בְּ "bet" found in both the Hebrew and Greek Lexicons with some incredible meanings. First we must address on point before we reveal the meanings in the word "In" written in Genesis 1:1. The preposition בְּ "bet" shows us that a temporal conjunction found in Genesis 2:4 shows us the account given to us in Genesis 1: 1-2 and Genesis 2:4 reveals the heavens and earth were already in existence. The preposition בְּ "bet" as shown in the Brown-Driver & Briggs Hebrew Lexicon page 91 to mean: *When they were created "in their being" sometimes it has in appearance the force of after that, but as a rule this is really due to the action denoted by the information being treated as extending over a period within which the action of the principal verb takes place.*

This is the generations (genealogical history) of the heavens and of the earth when they were created, in the day that Yahweh made the earth and the heavens.

Written by
Yibniyah Hawkins
5/27/2013

There is Nothing New Under the Sun

Gen 2:4 (KJV)

This shows us the heavens and the earth was already created when this historical account was documented. The reader should read the first verse with these understanding in mind.

"In the beginning (after) Yahweh had created the heavens and the earth. The earth became without form and empty; and darkness was upon the face of deep".

This is the preamble of the Government of Peace which states the purpose for creating a plan to save not only the earth from destruction, but also the entire universe. Let's return to the Hebrew preposition ב "bet" to discover what Yahweh reveals concerning the beginning.

 The Hebrew preposition ב "bet": is found in the Brown-Driver &Briggs Hebrew Lexicon page 88 to mean: The word **_In_** is arranged in three classes*: place, time and condition*.

The **place** denotes a position in a place preceded by a verb of motion. In the Greek the word #1722 "ἐv en" found in the Thayer's Greek-English Lexicon of the New Testament page 209 shows this 1. Locally of a Place in or on the surface of a place.

Time is shown in Hebrew preposition ב "bet" in the Brown-Driver &Briggs Hebrew Lexicon page 88 to mean: 5. Applied to time as Genesis 1:1 In the beginning 6. Denote a state or condition whether material or mental in which an action takes place. The Greek word for In ἐv en" found in the Greek-English Lexicon of the New Testament page 209 shows this: A notion of time, periods and portion s of time in which anything occurs in, on, at or during a time. It also signifies "an event"; at the time of this or that event. In the Manual Greek Lexicon of the New Testament by G.Abbot-Smith page 151 shows this to mean: "at the time of an event".

Condition is shown in Hebrew preposition ב "bet" in the Brown-Driver &Briggs Hebrew Lexicon page 88 to mean: 1. *a standard of measurement or computation* 2. A state or condition whether material or mental in which an action takes place; 3. Accompaniment and a instrument that co-exist; *Instrument; a sword etc… used*

There is Nothing New Under the Sun

as a efficient cause or instrumental cause; _The idea of accompaniment is instrumentality, an instrument , of or for ruling and effectuating_ **Fig. it used for marking a rule according to a manner, command or counsel.** The Greek word for "In" ἐv en" found in Thayer's Greek –English Lexicon of the New Testament page 209 to mean: A _condition in which anything is done or anyone acts and suffers. Denoting an instrument or means by or with which anything is accomplished owing to influence._

The word **_In_** written in Genesis 1:1 is revealing three important points the Government of Peace wants to make known to mankind. The place this history is describing is the earth and the visible heavens in which we reside "the Milk Way". In an ancient time period events occurred that caused some very disturbing conditions to develop in the both the heavens and the earth. In this time an instrument (weapon) was allowed to be created, that was instrumental in causing both the heavens and the earth to become desolate. This instrument (weapon) co-existed with the kingdoms of heavenly beings that trespassed, and came here to earth after Yahweh had created it. The weapons as they are today were keep in reserve in case of a need, and served to mark the rule, and superiority of an nation. These weapons of war were allowed by Yahweh to be created, and were instrumental in the account of the earth becoming without form and void, and darkness to be established on the face of deep. This as we will show was all planned by Yahweh who allowed all of this to develop for a reason that will become clear as we proceed. This weapon cause unthinkable destruction to the earth and the atmosphere we depend on for life. This event resulted in the foundation of the earth, which entails all the life giving function we depending on to be altered. This destruction was brought about by a counsel or assembly of nations who wanted to control the whole world. The results of this event are described in detail for us in Genesis 1:2. The instrument introduced by the Hebrew preposition "bet" is describe by the Hebrew words to be similar, but more powerful then the nuclear bombs we have today. The preamble which the Government of Peace is presenting to all mankind introduces former events designed to convince all nations today to consider their ways. Let's continue with the details of the former things (events) Yahweh commands us to proclaim to the nations. I

Written by
Yibniyah Hawkins
5/27/2013

There is Nothing New Under the Sun

admonish the reader to review the above information concerning this scripture which you must keep in mind as we proceed in this work.

In **the beginning** ;(*after)* Yahweh created the heaven and the earth.

Gen 1:1 (KJV)

Notice the meaning of the word *beginning* written in Genesis 1:1 is from the Hebrew word:

רִאשׁוֹן ri'shôn <u><H7223</u>— or *ri'shon*, ree-shone'; from <u><H7221></u> (ri'shah**); *first*,** in place, time or rank (as adjective or noun) :- **ancestors that were before (-time),** beginning, eldest, first, *former (thing), of old time, past*; former, before, foremost. **Aforetime**; proceeding

— Strong's Concordance

רִאשׁוֹן ri'shôn <u><H7223</u>— or *ri'shon*, ree-shone': is found in Brown-Driver & Briggs Hebrew and English Lexicon page 911 to mean: Former in time, former of two; former things i.e. former events; earlier predictions; from the beginning, the first of a definite series. Former state and former times.

When we use again one of the rules of Hebrew grammar used by the prophets to hide certain information from those who are not skilled in the ancient Hebrew art of writing we discover that by implementing one of the basic rules of Hebrew grammar a "**cipher**" known today as the "**invert cipher**". This is a cipher which rearranges the letters of the plain text in a different sequence. When this cipher is applied to the primitive root of the Hebrew word: רִאשׁוֹן ri'shôn which is the Hebrew word רֹאשׁ rō'sh the cipher render the Hebrew word: שָׁאַר shā'ar <u><H7604</u>. The Hebrew word:

שָׁאַר shā'ar <u><H7604</u>—found in Gesenius's Hebrew Lexicon by Samuel Tregell's page799:

Written by
Yibniyah Hawkins
5/27/2013

I. שָׁאַר TO BE LEFT, TO REMAIN, 1 Cr. 16:11. Arab. شَأَرَ. [In Thes. one meaning given is, *to be turgid, to swell up.*]

NIPHAL, pass. of Hiphil—(1) *to be let remain, to be left over*, Gen. 7:23; 42:38; 47:18; followed by a dat. to be left over to any one, Zec. 9:7. Part. *a survivor*, Eze. 6:12.

(2) *to remain* any where, Exo. 8:5, 7; Num. 11:26; *to remain*, Job 21:34, תְּשׁוּבֹתֵיכֶם נִשְׁאַר מָעַל "your answers remain perfidy," i. e. perfidious.

HIPHIL—(1) *to leave, to let remain*, Ex. 10:12; *to leave behind*, Joel 2:14; followed by a dat. to any one, Deu. 28:51.

(2) *to have left, to retain*, Nu. 21:35; Deu. 3:3. Derivatives, שְׁאָר, שְׁאֵרִית.

II. שָׁאַר i. q. שָׂאַר to ferment, whence מִשְׁאֶרֶת kneading trough (which see).

שְׁאָר (with Kametz impure) m. *rest, residue, remnant*, Isa. 10:20, 21, 22; 11:11; Zeph. 1:4.

There is yet another Hebrew word that results from this cipher and it is the Hebrew word:

אָשַׁר 'āshar <u><H833</u>— found in Gesenius's Hebrew Lexicon by Samuel Tregell's page 88:

אָשֵׁר or אָשַׁר (comp. pr. n. אָשֵׁר).

(1) TO BE STRAIGHT, RIGHT, i. q. יָשַׁר, especially used of a straight way, hence also of what is *upright, erect*, whence comes the signification of firmness and strength, in the Talmud.

(2) *to go straight on*, and generally *to go*, Pro. 9:6.

(3) *to be successful, to prosper, to be fortunate*, compare the kindred roots יָשַׁר No. 3, כָּשַׁר and עָשַׁר.

PIEL אִשֵּׁר—(1) *to guide*, or *lead straight*, Pro. 23:19; Isa. 1:17, אַשְּׁרוּ חָמוֹץ "lead the oppressor right," into the right way, (unless, comparing Pual No. 2, we render with the ancient versions, ῥύσασθε ἀδικούμενον. Vulg. *subvenite oppresso*, pr. *make the oppressed happy*), and generally *to lead*, Isa. 3:12;

There is a lot of information presented in this Hebrew word רִאשׁוֹן ri'shôn we will not be able to bring forth in this work. I revealed this because in this word beginning Yahweh is revealing a remnant of people who were left alive in this time period and they are document in the Hebrew text to have walk uprightly and reverence Yahweh only. The word beginning defined above also reveals there were ancestors that were before us in ancient times. This subject would require me to write concerning it in another work because I desire not to deviate further from this work. The scripture support what we are establishing in a few words. Remember earlier in the work Isaiah the prophet of Yahweh revealed in an ancient time Yahweh dried of the sea so a way was prepared for the ransomed to pass over! He also reveals in his work Yahweh laid down a charge to preserve and caused to continue amongst mankind the remembrance of the former events that occurred in an ancient time. Notice this from the following scripture

Awake, awake, put on strength, O arm of Yahweh; awake, as in the ancient days, in the generations of old. *Was is* not You Who cut Rahab, *and* wounded the dragon? *Was it* not you who dried the sea, the waters of the great deep; ***who made the depths of the sea a way for the ransomed to pass over?***

Isaiah 51:9-10 (KJV)

This is what Yahweh the King of Israel, and redeemer Yahweh of hosts says; I *am* the first, and I *am* the last; and beside me *there is* no source of power. And who, as I, shall call, and shall declare it, and set it in order for me, ***since I appointed the ancient people? And the things that are coming, and will come, let them show (fortell) them. Fear not, neither be afraid: have not I told you from that time, and have declared it? You are even my witnesses***. Is there a source of power beside me? Truly, *there is* no other; I know not *any*.

Isaiah 44:6-8 (KJV)

So we have learn from the word beginning written in Genesis 1:1 that Yahweh is speaking concerning former things which he has commission two witness to bear testimony of. He also reveals a remnant of people who he preserved in the beginning, to preserve and cause to be remembered the former events for a future time. Let's return once more to the word beginning there is still more knowledge hidden in this word that we must make known to the world. Notice again the Hebrew word:

ראשׁוֹן ri'shôn <H7223— or ***ri'shon***, ree-shone'; from <H7221> (ri'shah); *first*, in place, time or rank (as adjective or noun) :- ancestors that were before (-time), beginning, eldest, first, *former (thing), of old time, past*; former, before, foremost. Aforetime; preceding

Let's define some the words define in the Hebrew word "רִאשׁוֹן ri'shôn" notice the word *first* is defined in the Webster Dictionary page 723 with this meaning

First: Being before all others with respect of time; first thing before any else. 5, before some other event; the earliest; at the beginning or origin; **before or in preference to some *"proposed act or anticipated event"*.**

Fore: found in Webster Dictionary page 748 with this meaning: Preceding in place or time; **Antecedent.**

Antecedent: found in the Webster Dictionary page 87 with this meaning: A preceding event, or history. Something preliminary; a preliminary examination

Preliminary: found in the Webster Dictionary page 1525 with this meaning: nature of preparation or clearing away details which would encumber the main subject or problem; **also a preparatory movement intended to foreshadow; causing one to become acquaint with or gain knowledge of *something alleged*.**

Alleged: found in the Webster Dictionary page 55 with this meaning: To assert to be true without proving, alleged without proof are evidence which the evidence is to sustain. Alleged facts standing open to questioning or doubt; the opposing side advances a theory and adduces the strongest possible advance in its support.

Please notice that words are revealing Yahweh who the scripture shows in the beginning was warning the inhabitants of the earth in an ancient time of an event he predicted would transpire in their lives. Yahweh prior to this time period was warning the governments throughout the universe about the curses that were only alleged possibilities in the mind of these beings. He had no proof to support what he was strongly warning them against. They challenge Yahweh on the position that this was exiting only in his mind, and his warnings were not based on principles verifiable by either experiment or observation. They could not trust Yahweh's "prescience assertion" which he alone had the power to gain knowledge of events before they take place. There was no documented proof if one chooses to break the

Written by
Yibniyah Hawkins
5/27/2013

universal laws the curses, and destruction he warned them of would came upon them. This was the first undertaking to live a life of sin in opposition to Yahweh's Government of Peace. Yahweh through his infinite wisdom designed a plan to save creation and the universe from destruction. He put his plan into action when he created the earth and the visible heavens we call the Milk Way. Yahweh also through his ability to see the future knew these beings would rebelled against the laws of peace trespass and come to this planet he created to fulfill his plan of salvation. He used this time to gather knowledge and facts concerning the curses he foreknew would come upon all who would turn to a way of life which consisted of the mixer of righteousness and evil. He allowed a preliminary examination in which a preparatory act or event was allowed to be brought forth on earth amongst these heavenly beings. Yahweh used this time as a preparatory movement so he could have verifiable evidence of what he predicted with out any experimental knowledge or living proof. This is document in the Holy Writ as "the Great Experiment" designed to bring mankind and the rest of creation to a state of complete obedience. These former events were allowed to take place here on earth under the guidance of Yahweh. The prophet Isaiah was inspire to write this in the following scripture

That they may know from the rising of the sun, and from the west, that *there is* none beside me. I *am* Yahweh, and *there is* none else. ___I form the light, and create darkness: I make peace, and create destruction: I Yahweh do all these things.___

Isaiah 45:6-7 (KJV)

These former events were allowed so Yahweh could create on the new renovated earth a plan to create beings from mankind that will rule as he rules in total righteousness. This Great Experiment is shown to have been a scientific exhibit were information and facts were document from the observation of the events that were allowed to develop as the result of practicing a way of life consisting of both righteousness and evil. The inquiry and investigative evidence collected from this experiment was reduce to writing known to us as the ***"Testimony of Yahweh"*** which he gave to the children of Israyl. Notice this in the following scriptures:

There is Nothing New Under the Sun

Give ear, O my people, *to* My Law: incline your ears to the words of my mouth. I will open my mouth in a parable: I will utter dark sayings from ancient times: Which we have heard and known, and our fathers have told us. We will not hide *them* from our children, showing to the generation to come the praises of Yahweh, and his strength, and his wonderful works that he has done. ***For he established a testimony in Jacob***, and appointed a law in Israel, which he commanded our fathers, that they should make them known to their children: That the generation to come might know *them, even* the children *which* should be born; *who* should arise and declare *them* to their children: That they might set their hope in Yahweh, and not forget the works of our Heavenly Father, but keep his commandments:

Psalms 78:1-7 (KJV)

  Bind up the testimony; seal the law among my disciples.

Isaiah 8:16 (KJV)

To the law and to the testimony: if they speak not according to this word, *it is* because *there is* no light in them.

Isaiah 8:20 (KJV)

The law of Yahweh *is* perfect, converting the whole person: ***the testimony of Yahweh is sure, making the simple ones wise.***

Psalms 19:7 (KJV)

This experiment was designed to allow these beings to practice sin and experience as a result the curses they were warned against. This experiment (test) was designed to discover and illustrate a truth, that no one can live this way of life without causing destruction and death to abound. The only way Yahweh could remove the doubt prevailing amongst this group was to allow them to actually experience the effects of living this life of the mixer of righteousness and evil. These events were conducted under controlled testing and direct observations were the conditions that developed as a natural result of practicing sin were recorded. In this time Yahweh veiled his experiment from the rest of the universe this veil

Written by
Yibniyah Hawkins
5/27/2013

surrounded and enveloped the entire earth. This was done so he could later present his findings in a planned public exhibit of his findings, which he would present officially as evidence and as a solution to the corruption that all creation is subject to at this time.

This information I have presented concerning this ancient history was revealed to me by the use of an ancient code called the art of permutation. I have written concerning this art in many of my writings, and I would admonish the reader to visit our web-site www.eyesonthetruth.com, and click on the link entitle "An Unaltered Language" to learn more about this ancient code. I have decided in this work to focus on the content of the information revealed and ask the reader to prove to themselves wither I am wrong or right by studying the words, and history I have provided.

See, I have set before you this day life by righteousness, and death and destruction; I call heaven and earth to record (witness) this day against you, *that* I have set before you life and death, blessing and cursing: *Because you are free agents to make your own choice between righteousness and evil--* therefore choose life, that both you and your seed (children) may live:

Deut 30:15-19 (KJV)

This brings us to the former things Yahweh commanded to be preserved and remembered. We are commanded here to testify to the world these things as proof, and as a means to convince not only the nations of the earth, but also the universe. The inhabitant's of heaven are viewing the evidence obtained by "empirical knowledge" that Yahweh planned to be displayed as history unfolding here on earth through mankind. This way of life was presented to us in the book of Genesis which Eve participated in is described as "Rebellion" introduced to us as a tree of the mixer of righteousness and evil. This tree represented the ***"original undertaking to sin"*** that lead astray a huge number of heavenly beings turning them from Yahweh to a life of sin. Notice this in the following scripture:

Now the serpent was more subtle than any beast of the field which Yahweh had made. And he said unto the woman, Yea, has Yahweh said, Yes shall not eat of every tree of the garden? And the woman said unto the serpent, we may eat of the fruit of the trees of the garden: But of the fruit of the tree which *is* in the midst of the garden, Yahweh has said, ye shall not eat of it, neither shall ye touch it, lest ye die. And the serpent said unto the woman, ye shall not surely die: ***For Yahweh know that in the day you eat thereof, then your eyes shall be opened, and you shall be as gods, knowing righteousness and evil.***

Gen 3:1-5 (KJV)

In the above event Yahweh permitted this "undertaking" to be accepted by Eve who in turn caused Adam to accept this way of life. *This began the public exhibit of the evidence Yahweh had gather in an ancient time to be reiterated through mankind, and displayed to the universe as a public demonstration designed to prevent the re- occurrence of the destruction experience in a ancient time period*. This public exhibit of this way of life and its end result was designed to remove all reasonable doubt, and convince every living creature what Yahweh pre-warned them would come upon them if they reject his laws of peace.

We established earlier in this work that Yahweh predicted these former events before they take place in ancient times. He conducted an experiment designed to collect evidence he could used in a more advance education that he planned to be a public exhibit to the entire universe. This exhibit also involves building a holy family who would guide the universe away from death and destruction. Let's examine the details of the former things (events) recorded for us in his Holy Writ (scriptures). These events were preserved to convince the nation to consider the former things and to guide their lives way from sin which brings death, and choose a way of life that leads to righteousness and peace.

Let's return to Genesis 1:2 to examine the former events Yahweh commanded to be preserved for a future generation.

And the earth ***was without form, and void; and darkness was upon the face of the deep***. And the Spirit of Yahweh moved upon the face of the waters.

Gen 1:2 (KJV)

Written by
Yibniyah Hawkins
5/27/2013

There is Nothing New Under the Sun

The word **_was_** written in Genesis 1:2 is from the Hebrew word:

הָיָה hāyâ <H1961>—a primitive root [compare <H1933> (hava')]; to *exist*, i.e. *be* or *become, come to pass* (always emphatic, and not a mere copula or auxiliary) come (to pass), happen. Hamah: to become; to occur (verb indicates more than simple existence or identity; rather the verb makes a strong statement about the being or presence of a person or thing. Frequently translated it came to pass; Hayah emphasizes that the event really occurred; there existed total ruin and calamity.

Strong's Concordance

הָוָה hawâ <H1934—to *exist*; used in a great variety of applications (especially in connection with other words) :- be, become, came (to pass).

Strong's Concordance

הַוָּה hawwâ <H1942—< from> (hava') (in the sense of eagerly *coveting* and *rushing* upon; by implication of *falling*); *desire*; also *ruin*: - calamity, iniquity, mischief, mischievous (thing), perverse thing.—

Strong's Concordance

הָיָה hāyâ <H1961> Brown-Driver & Briggs Hebrew and English Lexicon page 226: Be; the idea of becoming. 1. Exist be in existence (of a continuous state or condition) be brought about.

The word **_was_** written in Genesis 1:2 should read in the verse: "The earth became without form" this shows us the earth was in existence before the calamity describe in the verse was brought about. The Hebrew word Hayah describes a **"frightful calamity"** that caused the earth to be without form. The phrase **_"without form"_** written in Genesis 1:2 is from the Hebrew word:

Written by
Yibniyah Hawkins
5/27/2013

תֹּהוּ tōhû <u><H8414></u>— from an unused root meaning to *lie waste; a desolation (of surface), i.e. desert; figurative a worthless thing; adverbial in vain: -* confusion, *empty place, without form, without order.*

—Strong's Concordance

תֹּהוּ tōhû <u><H8414></u>Brown-Driver & Briggs Hebrew Lexicon page 1062: Confusion, unreality; emptiness (primary meaning difficult to seize) of land reduced to primeval chaos and void (empty space). What is unreal; morally unreal; Hence desolate regions, ruins and destruction; sudden ruin.

The phrase *"without form"* is revealing the conditions and state of affairs on earth in the beginning. The conditions amongst the governments were of a brutal and cruel nature were they lack the ability to reason. This brutish nature lead to the devastation and ravaging of the earth and the atmosphere. In this time period covetousness was an accepted rule of action that was prevalent amongst the governments. The covetousness prevalent amongst the nations leads to war and fighting which caused the earth through wars to become a desolated waste place. The nations in this ancient time period refused to submit to a righteous order (system of government) who could have guided and instruct them in the laws of peace.

Let's return to Genesis 1:2:

And the earth *was (became) without form, and void; and darkness was upon the face of the deep*. And the Spirit of Yahweh moved upon the face of the waters.

Gen 1:2 (KJV)

The word *void* written in Genesis 1:2 is from the Hebrew word:

בֹּהוּ bōhû <u><H922></u>— from an unused root (meaning to *be empty*); **a vacuity**, i.e. **An undistinguishable *ruin***: - emptiness, **an empty space**; a void of the **primeval earth.**

—Strong's Concordance

There is Nothing New Under the Sun

This word **"void"** is revealing a great secret concerning the condition the earth was brought to. We have establish above the surface of the earth was laid waste and desolate of all life. The Government of Yahweh know reveals the earth became void of a portion of its upper atmosphere. Notice with me some of the words define in the Hebrew word "bohu".

Vacuity: Webster Dictionary page 1069: The state of being a vacuum; emptiness; a vacant space; void; 2. Lack of intelligence; stupidity

Vacuum: Webster Dictionary page 1069: a space left empty as by the removal of something. **A space absolutely devoid of matter**. 2. *A partial diminution of the normal atmospheric pressure.*

Primeval: Webster Dictionary page: The first ages of the earth; a young earth. Constituting a beginning; existing at or from the very beginning.

The word "void" is revealing that a portion of the expanse (firmament) was removed creating a vacuum effect within the earth. The Hebrew word "bohu" is describing the removal of something which creates empty space void of matter. This is also describe by the Government of Yahweh as **an undistinguishable** *ruin* meaning in there pursuit of military dominance over other nations the manipulation of the atmosphere and removal of the ionosphere brought devastating storms in the form of tornadoes, earthquakes, hurricanes and scorching heat.

We understand this today because of the research conducted by our governments through a program called HAARP *(High Frequency Active Aurora Research Project).* Through this project the governments have learned how to manipulate the electro-magnetic field lines that wrap around the earth, and also the ionosphere. The scientists today have only look at the atmospheric system as an unconnected system. They have failed to look at this system as integrated whole which is effected by any *"alteration or external forcing"* produce by man. The ionosphere is about 30 miles above the earth stretching out into space it is a highly charged area which filters cosmic radiation and is essential for life to exist on earth. The HAARP project uses antennas that direct radio frequency energy straight into the upper atmosphere affecting the electromagnetic field lines causing them to reverse their course. The electromagnetic field lines normally move in a south to north direction when they are manipulated by radio frequency energy, it moves in a reverse direction from north to south. This causes the electromagnetic field lines to move in a spiral motion creating as it wraps around the earth a _"shield"_ that is designed to destroy incoming missiles and asteroids that could potentially destroy the earth. They have also discovered side effects to their research when the ionosphere is heated by their "ionospheric heaters" it causes the ionosphere to be lifted up and moved out of its place pushing it further above the earth. _They understand now that by moving this much of the atmosphere further above the earth causes the higher and lower pressure systems to become altered.__**(Remember above in the definition were it show a partial diminution of the normal atmospheric pressure.)**_

   It also alters along with the higher and lower pressure systems the **"jet streams"** which causes a down stream weather effect generating destructive storms. This technology will cause a major portion of the upper atmosphere to moved out of it normal space by pushing it further above the earth. This creates the empty space (void) Yahweh informs us of in Genesis 1:2. The expanse (firmament) was one of the first things Yahweh set in order when he renovated both the heavens and the earth. This empty space creates a vacuum effect causing an alteration in lower regions of the atmosphere below the ionosphere. It's important we understand once you remove one portion of the atmosphere something has to take its place. The lower portion of the atmosphere is forced to be altered creating a vacuum effect forcing the void space to be filled. Yahweh who renovated the earth in the beginning caused to remain evidence of the disturbances and destruction of the heavens and the earth. Yahweh caused to exist according to his plan for this evidence to remain, so his anointed one could give testimony concerning the former things. This evidence is preserved for us in the visible heavens we exist in called the Milk Way.

Written by
Yibniyah Hawkins
5/27/2013

There is Nothing New Under the Sun

The earth along with the planets in our solar system under went some dramatic changes causing these planets to become desolate of all life. The scripture describes them as "old waste places" that Yahweh has plans to rebuild (renovate) and give as an inheritance to the 144,000 priestly kings. This men and women will be made in Yahweh's image and given authority to rebuild these places restoring all the life given functions in these planets. These planets in our solar system serve today as evidence of the destruction that transpired in both the heavens and earth. The planet serving as an example of the destruction written in Genesis 1:2 that occurred on earth before Yahweh renovated it is the planet Venus. Let's review some of the evidence our scientist have discovered recently that leaves them perplexed concerning Venus's atmosphere, and the activities occurring within this planet. Notice this in the following information:

In the grand scheme of the solar system, Venus and Earth are almost the same distance from the sun. Yet the planets differ dramatically: Venus is some 100 times hotter than Earth and its days more than 200 times longer. "***The atmosphere on Venus is so thick that the longest any spacecraft has survived on its surface before being crushed is a little over two hours***". ***There's another difference, too. Earth has a magnetic field and Venus does not – a crucial distinction when assessing the effects of the sun on each planet.***

Venus has no such protective shield, but it is still an immovable rock surrounded by an atmosphere that disrupts and interacts with the solar wind, causing interesting space weather effects.

A recent study, appearing online in the Journal of Geophysical Research on February 29, 2012, has found clear evidence on Venus for a type of space weather outburst quite common at Earth, called "***a hot flow anomaly***". These anomalies, also known as HFAs, ***cause a temporary reversal of the solar wind that normally moves past a planet. An HFA surge causes the material to flood backward, says David Sibeck, a scientist at NASA's Goddard Space Flight Center in Greenbelt, Md., who studies HFAs at Earth and is a co-author on the paper.***

Written by
Yibniyah Hawkins
5/27/2013

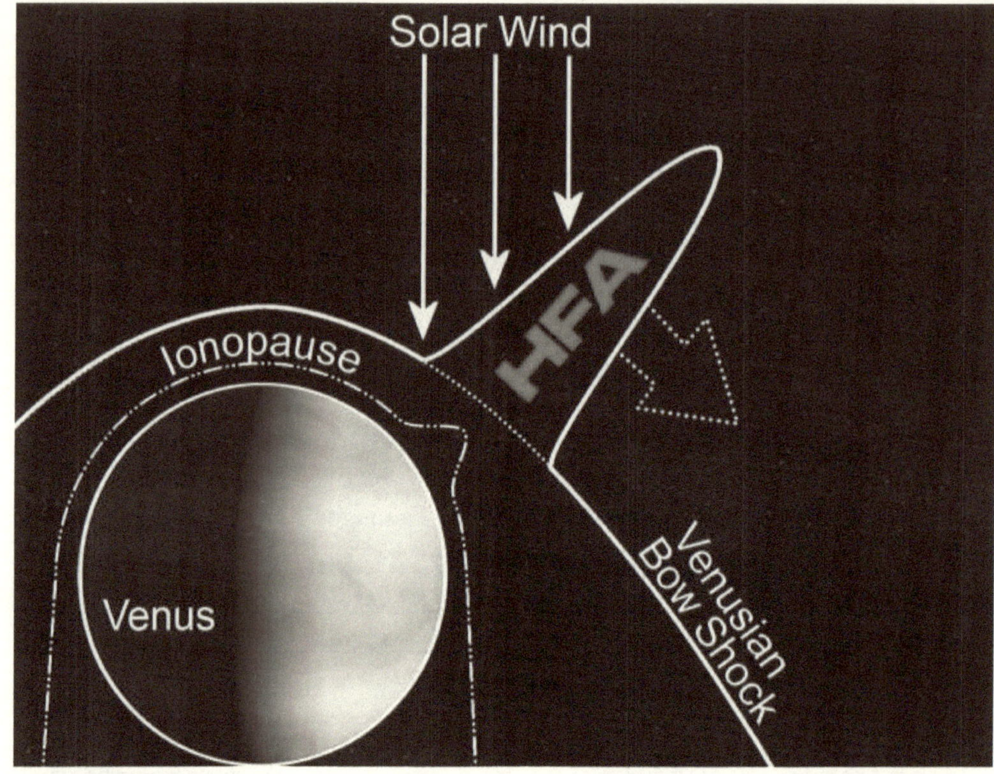

› View larger
when discontinuities in the solar wind remain in contact with a planet's bow shock, they can collect a pool of hot particles that becomes a hot flow anomaly (HFA). An HFA on Venus most likely acts like a "vacuum", pulling up parts of the planet's atmosphere. Credit: NASA/Collinson

With no magnetic field to interact with, space weather at Venus is milder than that at Earth, but occurs much closer to the surface.

By taking the Venus Express data and comparing it to the known physics at Earth, the scientists painted a possible picture of how an HFA forms at Venus. *"The*

Written by
Yibniyah Hawkins
5/27/2013

moving solar wind with its attendant magnetic fields harbors discontinuities, areas where the magnetic fields change direction, sharply and abruptly". **The bow shock on Venus serves as the boundary between the incoming solar wind, and the planets own ionosphere – a layer of atmosphere filled with charged particles.** This boundary changes in height easily in response to the environment, and so the scientists believe it would also respond strongly in the presence of an HFA. *"Since the HFA causes material to flow sunward, away from the planet, it may operate almost like a vacuum cleaner, pulling that bow shock further away from Venus. The size of the ionosphere would swell in concert."*

Karen C. Fox
NASA Goddard Space Flight Center, *Greenbelt, MD*

Each Friday this summer, Life's Little Mysteries, *a sister site to Live Science, presents The Greatest Mysteries of the Cosmos, starting with our solar system.*

Although the second planet from the sun is named after the Roman goddess of love, Venus is anything but lovely, at least from a hospitality perspective. For starters, its surface temperature pushes **"900 degrees Fahrenheit"**, making Venus the hottest planet in the solar system.

It gets worse: *"A thick shroud of carbon dioxide presses down with 92 times the pressure of Earth's atmosphere on a bone-dry landscape". The "opaque clouds" that block our view of the world's surface are laced with sulfuric acid.*

As you might imagine, studying Venus has proved difficult. But bit by bit, scientists are learning more about Earth's closest planetary neighbor. Here are some of the biggest mysteries regarding the brightest object in our sky after the sun and the moon.

Climate gone to ruin

Written by
Yibniyah Hawkins
5/27/2013

There is Nothing New Under the Sun

Venus is sometimes referred to as Earth's "evil twin." In terms of size, composition and orbital location, hellish Venus is actually the planet that's most similar to our own (that we know of). ***Early in Venus' history, scientists think, the world was probably a lot like Earth, with oceans and a much cooler climate***.

Figuring out exactly when and how Venus became a furnace will help with modeling Earth's changing climate, as well as avoiding the possibility of sharing Venus' fate.

Spinning backwards

All of the planets in the solar system orbit the sun in a counterclockwise direction when viewed from the sun's North Pole, and nearly all spin in this same direction on their axes. Not so on Venus, which has retrograde rotation (Uranus does this, too). On Venus, in other words, "the sun rises in the west and sets in the east."

This clockwise spin is probably the result of a cosmic collision early in Venus' history. *This story was provided by Life's Little Mysteries, a sister site to LiveScience. Follow Life's Little Mysteries on Twitter @llmysteries, and then join us on Facebook*

We revealed early that in an ancient time the effects of these alterations were described as an ***"undistinguishable ruin"*** not attracting notice or attention. The effects of the alteration were only realized when the destruction in the form of destructive storms started ravaging the earth.

When the Hebrew word **"בֹּהוּ bōhû"** for the word void written in Genesis 1:2 is reduced to its root words, and the art of permutation is applied to the Hebrew words reveals some remarkable information. These root words are found in the Hebraic Tongue Restored by Fabre de Olivet pages 302,329

Written by
Yibniyah Hawkins
5/27/2013

בה BH. Onomatopoetic root which depicts the noise made by a thing being opened, and which, representing it *yawning*, offers to the imagination the idea of *a chasm, an abyss*, etc.

בהו *An abyss*, a thing whose depth cannot be fathomed, physically as well as morally. See הה.

The Arabic به, as onomatopoetic root characterizes astonishment, surprise. The Arabic word بهي which is formed from it, designates that which is astonishing, surprising; that which causes admiration. به signifies to be *resplendent*, and بهي *glorious*.

The word **_chasm_** defined in the above root word is found in the Webster Dictionary page 350: A marked interruption of continuity; a gap 4. A sundering breach of relation; creating a divergence between people and things.

Divergence: defined in the Webster Dictionary page 574: The act, fact or amount of diverging 2. Variation, deviation and separation. 3. To move, lie; **_extend in a different direction from a common point; to have no unique limit._**

The Hebrew word for void "בֹהוּ bōhû" is describing an obvious interruption in continuity and connection of the upper and lower atmospheres. Notice the following roots for the Hebrew word "bohu".

Written by
Yibniyah Hawkins
5/27/2013

הו   HOU.   The sign of life united to the convertible sign, image of the knot which binds nothingness to being, constitutes one of the roots most difficult to conceive that any tongue can offer. It is the potential life, the power of being, the incomprehensible state of a thing which, not yet existing, is found, nevertheless, with *power of existing.* Refer to the notes.

The Arabic roots هَا, هُو, هَه, ي having lost nearly all the general and universal ideas developed by the analogous Hebraic roots, and conserving nothing of the intellectual, with the sole exception of the pronominal relation هُو in which some traces are still discoverable, are restricted to the particular acceptations of the root היה, of which I have spoken above: so that they have received for the most part a baleful character. Thus هُوَ has designated that which is cowardly, weak and pusillanimous; هُوي that which is unstable, ruinous; the verb هوي has signified *to pass on, to die, to cease being.* The word هوا which designated originally potential existence, designates only *air, wind, void;* and this same existence, degraded and materialized more and more in صهواء has been the synonym of *hell.*

הוה   This root materialized expresses *a nothingness, an abyss of evils, a frightful calamity.*

The above roots describe for us once the void is caused to exist there is a incomprehensible state of things which has the power of existing as the result of lifting the ionosphere further into space causing as a result *"frightful calamites"* to occur on earth . Notice the meaning of the word *"calamity"* defined in the above definition is found in the Webster Dictionary with this meaning:

Calamity: Webster Dictionary page294: *Great misfortune or disaster as a flood etc. 2 Grievous affliction; adversity, and misery. Syn: cataclysm, catastrophe*

Cataclysm: Webster Dictionary page 325: *A sudden and violent physical action producing changes in the earth's surface 3. Any earth-shaking change.*

Catastrophe: Webster Dictionary page326: *Sudden and widespread disaster 3. A final event or conclusion usually a unfortunate one; a disastrous end.4 A sudden and violent disturbance especially of the earth's surface.*

Disaster: Webster Dictionary page 561: *A calamitous event, esp. one occurring suddenly and causing great loss of life, damage and hardship; something caused by carelessness, negligence, bad judgment or the like; or by natural forces as hurricanes or floods.*

When the art of permutations are applied to the Hebrew word בֹּהוּ bōhû it reveals these etymological root words. These are found in the Hebraic Tongue Restored by Fabre de Olivet pages 388-389 & 346

בֹּה **The sign of exterior and passive action united to that of elementary labour, or to the root אֶת, symbol of all equality, constitutes a root to which are attached the ideas of abolition, desuetude; of ravage carried on by time, by the action of the elements, or by man; thence,**

Written by
Yibniyah Hawkins
5/27/2013

מחה   Action of *effacing, depriving, taking away, de-stroying;* of *razing* a city, an edifice; of *washing, cleansing,* etc.

הא   HA. Root is analogous with the root חי, which bears the real character of the sign ח. This is used more under its onomatopoetic relation, to denote the violence of an effort, a blow struck, an exclamatory cry.

Let's define the meaning of the some of the words defined in the above roots to get a greater understanding of what occurred in the beginning.

<u>Abolition</u>: found in the Webster Dictionary page 2 with this meaning: 1. *utter destruction; annulment; to bring to nothing*

<u>Desuetude</u>: Webster Dictionary page 206: *To be accustomed to disuse; as the laws falling into desuetude; the discontinuance of use or practice of; to be no longer used; to be disaccustomed to, and unlearned.*

<u>Ravage</u>: Webster Dictionary page616: *the act or practice of violently destroying 2. Ruin; devastating damage; to destroy violently.*

<u>Elements</u>: Webster Dictionary page 242: *The first and basic principles; 2. <u>the forces of the atmosphere; climate.</u>*

The word "**void**" is describing for us the state of affairs, and the conditions prevalent in the earth in the beginning. The inhabitance of the earth at that time became accustomed to misusing, disusing, and no longer practicing the laws of peace. They no longer look to the laws of peace to guide them in their pursuits, but instead they endeavored to live a life of sin in disobedience to Yahweh. This resulted in wars abounding in the earth and the foundations of the earth were altered because of their technological advancements. This disturbance of the foundations of the earth caused widespread destruction on the earth. This was caused by the altering of the forces of the atmosphere which caused the atmosphere to act violently laying waste the surface of the earth. The earth brought about violent earthquakes, droughts, the ice age, tsunamis, tornadoes, and hurricanes which ravages the earth. This was shown by Yahweh to be carried out over the spanned of many years were the destructive changes grew worst eventually causing the earth to become worthless, and void of its life giving functions. Let's continue in Genesis 1: 2:

In the beginning Yahweh created the heaven and the earth. And the earth became without form, and void; and ***darkness was upon the face of the deep***. And the Spirit of Yahweh moved upon the face of the waters.

Gen 1:1-2 (KJV)

The word "darkness" written in Genesis 1:2 is from the Hebrew word:

חֹשֶׁךְ ḥōshek <u><H2822</u>—from <u><H2821></u> (chashak); the *dark*; hence (literal) *darkness*; figurative *misery, **destruction, death, ignorance, sorrow, wickedness*** :- dark (-ness), night, **obscurity**—Strong's Concordance

חָשַׁךְ ḥāshak <u><H2821></u>—a primitive root; **to *be dark* (as *withholding* light)**; transitive **to *darken* :- be black, be (make) dark, darken, cause darkness, be dim, hide.**

—Strong's Concordance

When the art of permutations are applied to the Hebrew word "חֹשֶׁךְ ḥōshek" it reveals two important aspects that transpired here on earth. First it describes the effects the alterations had on the atmosphere of the earth, causing it to not receive the benefits of sun light which eventually lead to the darkness described here in Genesis. This darkness was the result of the earth being moved out of its place causing the earth to experience a time when a large portion of the earth was covered with ice. Notice with me some of the details concerning the alteration recorded for us in the beginning.

Written by
Yibniyah Hawkins
5/27/2013

סב‎ 8B. When this root is conceived as the product of the circumferential sign united to that of interior

action ב‎, it expresses every idea of occasional force, cause, reason: but when it is the root אב‎, image of every conceivable fructification, joined by contraction to this same sign, then this root is applied to that which surrounds, circumscribes, envelops.

The Arabic سب‎ contains in general all the acceptations of the Hebraic root; but inclining toward those which are more particularized in a physical sense than in a moral one.

סב‎ Every kind of *contour, circuit, girdle; a circumstance, an occasion, a cause.*

The Arabic سبب‎ has the same sense; but the primitive root سب‎ having deviated toward the physical, signifies *to distort* a thing, to take the wrong side; *to curse* someone, *to injure* him, etc.

סב‎ and סבב‎ (*intens.*) Action of *turning, going round, circuiting, enveloping, circumventing, warning, converting, perverting,* etc.

The Arabic سب‎ signifies *to put* a thing *upside down; to pour out, upset.*

The above roots describe a *"girdle"* enveloping the earth moving around the planet in a circular manner. It also describes the girdle as being distorted and is the cause of something. Notice the meaning of the word girdle:

<u>Girdle</u>: found in the Webster Dictionary page 317: *A belt; anything that surrounds or encircles. 2. To surround or bind as with a girdle; to moving around something in a circle.*

This girdle is describing our atmosphere and the electromagnetic field lines that surround the planets in our galaxy. Let's continue with the root words revealed by the art of permutation.

בב **SS.** The circumferential sign being added to itself, constitutes a root which denotes in an intensive manner every eccentric movement tending to increase a circle and give it a more extended diameter: thence, every idea of going away from the centre, of emigration, travel: thence,

סר **SR.** The circumferential sign joined to that of movement proper, constitutes a root whence issue all ideas of disorder, perversion, contortion, apostasy; also those of force, audacity, return, education, new direction,

סת **STH.** Every kind of mutual, sympathetic covering, every kind of veil, of darkness. The Arabic ست

Written by
Yibniyah Hawkins
5/27/2013

עֲבׂ HB. The sign of material sense united by contraction to the root אֲבׂ, symbol of all covetous desire and all fructification, constitutes a root which hieroglyphically characterizes the material centre: it is, in a less general sense, that which is condensed, thickened; which becomes heavy and dark.

The Arabic عَبَ signifies properly *to charge with a burden;* by غَبَ, is understood *to finish, to draw to an end, to become putrid.*

עֲבׂ Every idea of *density, darkness; a cloud, a thick vapour; a plank, a joist.*

עֲבׂ Action of being *condensed, thickened,* of becoming *palpable, cloudy, sombre, opaque;* etc. See אֲבׂ of which עֲבׂ is the degeneration and intensifying.

עד HD. The sign of material sense, contracted with the root אד, symbol of relative unity, image of every emanation and every division, constitutes a very important root which, hieroglyphically, develops the idea of *time*, and of all things temporal, sentient, transitory. Symbolically and figuratively it is worldly voluptuousness, sensual pleasure in opposition to spiritual pleasure; in a more restricted sense, every limited period, every periodic return.

The Arabic عد, which is related in general, to the radical sense of the Hebrew, signifies in particular, *to count, number, calculate*, etc.; the word غد, the time which follows the actual time; *tomorrow*.

עד *The actual time;* a fixed point in time or space expressed by the relations *to, until, near*: a same state continued, a temporal duration, expressed in like manner by, *now, while, still;* a periodic return as *a month;* a thing *constant, certain, evident, palpable*, by which one can give testimony; *a witness.*

עד or עדד (*intens.*) Continued time furnishes the idea of *eternity, stability, constancy;* thence, the action of *enacting, constituting, stating*, etc.

עוד Action of returning periodically furnishes the idea of *evidence, certitude;* action of returning unceasingly,

Let's define some of the words in the above root words:

Contortion: Webster Dictornary page 164: *To force out of shape as by twisting, wrenching etc. distort.*

Written by
Yibniyah Hawkins
5/27/2013

There is Nothing New Under the Sun

<u>Condense</u>: Webster Dictionary page 157: *To make more dense or compact; <u>compress;</u> to change to a denser form; pass into a denser form.*

<u>Density</u>: Webster Dictionary page 202: *The state or quality of being dense; compact; closely set or crowed condition. 2. Thick and impenetrable; relatively opaque; transmitting little light.*

These root words above are revealing the scientific phenomena our scientists are seeing today in our own atmosphere, and in planets like Venus throughout the Milk Way. The etymological root words reveal in an ancient time period there was an internal forcing that caused an eccentric movement of our atmosphere. The intent was as it is today to utilize the forces of the earth for military purposes. The eccentric movement caused the atmosphere to increase its diameter which resulted in the upper atmosphere extending above the earth. This caused the upper atmosphere to operate in an irregular manner. The internal forcing which is the manipulation of the forces in the upper atmosphere is an ***<u>"illegal action"</u>*** according to the ordinances that govern the earth. This manipulation of the electromagnetic field lines which circle the earth caused as we saw above a destructive twisting or spiral motion. This ancient history shown in the etymological roots words describes a drastic change in the upper atmosphere which caused it to be **"condense and thicken"** creating a mass of obscuring clouds which enveloped the earth preventing the sun from shining on earth. This created a veil of thick darkness that could be felt and realized instantly. Notice the following information taken from a work I wrote entitle "In that Day the Lights in Heaven will be Darken" www.eyesonthetruth.com

The above information is describing two important process one transpiring in a region of the upper atmosphere called the thermosphere shown here to be reversing its usual function and now contracting; causing a mass of particles to unite, resulting in a important area of the atmosphere to undergo a change. The change will be excited by a condition of cooling in the thermosphere, therefore

There is Nothing New Under the Sun

obstructing the ability of light to shine here on earth. The Milk Way is shown by our scientist to be moving into a highly energized region in the universe, causing our galaxy to heat-up dramatically. The above abnormal contracting described above was reported by a NASA scientist in 2010 notice this from the following information entitled "Scientists baffled by unusual upper atmosphere shrinkage"

*An upper **layer of Earth's atmosphere recently shrank** so much that researchers are at a loss to adequately explain it, NASA said on Thursday.*

The thermosphere, which blocks harmful ultraviolet rays, expands and contracts regularly due to the sun's activities. As carbon dioxide increases, it has a cooling effect at such high altitudes, which also contributes to the contraction.

But even these two factors aren't fully explaining the extraordinary contraction which, though unlikely to affect the weather, can affect the movement of satellites, researchers said.

*"**This is the biggest contraction of the thermosphere in at least 43 years**," John Emmert of the Naval Research Lab was quoted as saying in NASA news report.*

Emmert is the lead author of a paper announcing the finding in the June 19 issue of the journal Geophysical Research Letters.

*"We cannot explain the **abnormally low densities**, which are about 30 percent lower" than from previous contractions, Emmert told CNN.com.*

The thermosphere lies high above Earth's surface, close to where the atmosphere ends and space begins. It ranges in altitude from 55 miles (90km) to 370 miles (600km) above the ground -- the realm of meteors, auroras, space shuttles and the international space station. This is the biggest contraction of the thermosphere in at least 43 years. The thermosphere interacts strongly with the sun and hence is greatly influenced by the sun's solar activity, which occurs in cycles.

*By **Derrick Ho**, Special to CNN*
July 17, 2010 12:07 a.m. EDT

Written by
Yibniyah Hawkins
5/27/2013

There is Nothing New Under the Sun

This contraction and low density is shown to have created a mass of dark clouds which surrounded the earth blocking the sun, and causing a darkness that could be felt. This darkness is similar to the darkness recorded in the days of Mosheh. Notice this in the following scriptures.

And Yahweh said unto Moses, **Stretch out your hand toward _heaven_**, that there **_may be darkness over the land of Egypt, even darkness which may be felt_**. And Moses stretched forth his hand toward heaven; and there was a **_"thick darkness in all the land of Egypt three days:"_**

Ex 10:21-22 (KJV)

The word **heaven** written here in Exodus 10:21 is from the Hebrew word:

שָׁמַיִם shāmayim <u><H8064></u>— dual of an unused singular **shameh**, shaw-meh'; from an unused root meaning to _be lofty_; the _sky_ (as _aloft_; the dual perhaps alluding to the visible arch in which the clouds move, as well as to the higher ether where the celestial bodies revolve):- air, × astrologer, heaven (-s).Shameh: Introduction: Signifes the atmosphere immediately surrounding the earth. It also refers to the vast expanse through which the stars are moving in their courses.

 The New Strong's Expanded Exhaustive Concordance of the Bible Red-Letter Edition

The above scripture proves to us the darkening phenomenal was a direct result of a change in the upper atmosphere. The above etymological root words show Yahweh caused to remain as evidence of this destruction in an ancient time the **_"periodic re-occurrence of earth-shaking climate disturbances we are experiencing"_**. The earth over the course of 6,000 years now has experience cycles of climate changes

Written by
Yibniyah Hawkins
5/27/2013

There is Nothing New Under the Sun

in form of destructive storms, droughts, earthquakes and hurricanes. This is shown by Yahweh to continue until an appointed time when a witness will reveal the former events in an attempt to prevent the reoccurrence of the destruction that caused the earth to become desolate waste place. This destruction is shown in the history of the heavens and the earth recorded for us in Genesis to have also caused widespread destruction in our own galaxy. The planets in our galaxy are shown to have become desolated waste places. This is very evident when one examines the uninhabitable planets in our galaxy. These planets were once full of life, until they were trespass upon by powerful beings, which the scripture show caused the foundations of both heaven and earth to be destroyed. Notice this in the following scriptures:

Have you not known? Have you not heard? ***Has it not been told you from the beginning?*** Have you not understood from the foundations of the earth? *It is* He (*Yahweh*) that ***sits above the circle of the earth***, and ***the inhabitants*** thereof *are* as grasshoppers; He stretches out the heavens like a curtain, and spreads them out as a tent to dwell in:

Isaiah 40:21-22 (KJV)

If the reader will notice that Isayah reveals that the universe is filled with people and planets *(dwelling places)*. The term used ***above "its inhabitants are like grasshoppers"*** is used here to describe a huge number of people that are residing in the universe. Please read the following scripture which proves the use of the phrase to mean a huge number.

For they came up with their cattle and their tents, and t***hey came as grasshoppers for multitude; for both they and their camels were without number:***

Judges 6:5 (KJV)

And the Midianites and the Amalekites and all the children of the east lay along in ***the valley like grasshoppers for multitude; and their camels were without number, as the sand by the sea side for multitude.***

Judges 7:12 (KJV)

Written by
Yibniyah Hawkins
5/27/2013

There is Nothing New Under the Sun

Now notice the destruction this begins caused in the earth and the visible heavens.

Yahweh stands in the assembly of the mighty; he judges among the gods. How long will you judge unjustly, and accept the persons of the wicked? Selah. You *should* defend the poor and fatherless: do justice to the afflicted and needy.
 Deliver the poor and needy: rid *them* out of the hand of the wicked. You know nothing, you understand nothing; you walk about in darkness: and all the foundations of the earth are out of course because of you.
 I have said, Ye *are* gods; and all of you *are* children of the Most High.

 But ye shall die like men*(mankind),* and fall like all the rulers of the earth.

Psalms 82:1-7 (KJV)

For this what Yahweh of hosts says: Once again , in a little while, and I will shake the heavens, and the earth, and the sea, and the dry *land*;

Hag 2:6 (KJV)

Let's return to Genesis 1:2 to continue with the former events that occurred here on earth.

Now the earth became without form, and void; and darkness *was* upon the ___*face of the deep.*___ And the Spirit of Yahweh moved upon the face of the waters.

Gen 1:2 (KJV)

The word "face" written in Genesis 1:2 is from the Hebrew word:

פָּנֶה pāneh <u><H6440</u>— found in The Brown-Driver-Briggs Hebrew and English Lexicon page 816 shows this word to mean: **The face= surface of ground; refers also to the condition, state of a thing, as denoted by its appearance; the appearance(situation, attitude) of the affair.**

פָּנֶה **pāneh:** Gesenius's Hebrew and Chaldee Lexicon of Old Testament by Samuel Prideaux Tregelles page 679 with this meaning: *The face, the surface of a thing; of the earth and the waters. Hence; the external appearance, state, and condition.*

Written by
Yibniyah Hawkins
5/27/2013

Used of time; front, before of old; anciently. Before is used of time (of surface of the water; out upon, over the surface.

When the art of permutation is applied to the Hebrew word "פָּנֶה pāneh" face, it shows us the conditions existing on earth at that time. This word reveals frightful calamities that continued over many years by wars and fighting, and by the forces of the atmosphere causing destructive storms. The drastic forms of changes in the climate caused devastating storms to be stirred upon land and the seas. When the **"invert cipher"** is applied to the Hebrew word "פָּנֶה pāneh" it reveals the Hebrew word:

נָפָה nāpâ <u><H5299></u>— from <u><H5130></u> (nuwph) in the sense of *__lifting__*; a *height*; also a *__border, coast, and region__*.

—Strong's Concordance

נוּף nûp <u><H5130></u>— a primitive root; to *quiver* (i.e. *vibrate* up and down, or *rock* to and fro); used in a great variety of applications: - lift up, move, shake, and wave.

Strong's Concordance

This is speaking of a coastal region were an earthquake caused a region to be elevated and also caused the sea to be agitated. The word face also describes a mass of water from the seas submerging the earth under water. Notice this from the following etymological root words derived from the art of permutations.

ים IM. The sign of manifestation united to that of exterior action as collective sign, composes a root whose purpose is to indicate universal manifestation and to develop all ideas of mass and accumulation.

Written by
Yibniyah Hawkins
5/27/2013

םׄ   In a literal and restricted sense, *the sea;* that is to say, the universal aqueous manifestation, the mass of waters.

As noun, the Arabic ﻊ , signifies *the sea,* and as verb, *to submerge.* This word is preserved in the Coptic ΦΙΟΜ, and appears not to be foreign to the Japanese *umi.*

The earth was caused at this time to move to and fro with a violent earthquake that is described above as lifting up the waters of a coastal region of the earth. Let' return to Genesis 1:2 to understand how the earth becomes submerge under a mass of water.

And the earth was without form, and void; and darkness *was* upon the face of the *deep*. And the Spirit of Yahweh moved upon the face of the waters.

Gen 1:2 (KJV)

The word "deep" written in Genesis 1:2 is from the Hebrew word:

תְּהוֹם tehôm <u><H8415</u>— or **tehom**, teh-home'; (usually feminine) from <u><H1949></u> (huwm); an **abyss (as a surging mass of water), especially the deep (the main sea** or the subterranean *water-supply*):- deep (place), **depth.**

—Strong's Concordance

הוּם hûm <u><H1949</u>— a primitive root [compare <u><H2000></u> (hamam)]; ***to make uproar, or agitate greatly: -*** destroy, move, make a noise.

—Strong's Concordance

Written by
Yibniyah Hawkins
5/27/2013

הָמַם hāmam <H2000>— a primitive root [compare <H1949> (huwm), <H1993> (hamah)]; ***properly to put in commotion***; by implication to *disturb, drive, destroy*: - consume, crush, destroy, discomfit, trouble, and vex.

—Strong's Concordance

תְּהוֹם tehôm: found in the Gesenius's Hebrew and Chaldee Lexicon to Old Testament by Samuel Prideaux Tregelles page 857:

תְּהוֹם pl. תְּהֹמוֹת comm., a poetic word, pr. water making a noise, in commotion (from the root הוּם), hence — (1) *wave* (Welle, Woge), Psa. 42:8, תְּהוֹם אֶל־תְּהוֹם קֹרֵא "wave calleth unto wave," i. e. wave follows wave without intermission. Pl. Ex. 15:5, 8; Ps. 33:7; 78:15.

(2) *a great quantity of waters*, i. q. מַיִם Deut. 8:7; Eze. 31:4; תְּהוֹם רַבָּה *ocean, sea*, Gen. 7:11; Ps. 36:7; Am. 7:4; and simply תְּהוֹם id., Job 28:14; 38:16, 30. Hence —

(3) *gulf, abyss*, even used of the deep hollows of the earth, Ps. 71:20. (Syr. ܬܗܘܡܐ wave, abyss.)

The word ***"deep"*** is describing an excitement and agitating of the sea causing it to swell bringing a great quantity of water upon the dry land. This is described as an overwhelming mass of waves which came upon the land destroying everything in its sight. The Hebrew word "תְּהוֹם tehôm" when reduced to its etymological roots reveals the cause of the agitation of the sea. Notice this in the following Hebrew root word derived from the Hebrew word: "תְּהוֹם **tehôm**":

Written by
Yibniyah Hawkins
5/27/2013

These root words are found in the Hebraic Tongue Restored by Fabre de Olivet 331-332

חֵם **HEM. Universalized life: the vital power of the universe. See** הו.

הֵם **Onomatopoetic and idiomatic root, which indicates every kind of tumultuous noise, commotion, fracas.**

The Arabic هم **characterizes, in general, that which is heavy, painful, agonizing. It is literally** *a burden, care, perplexity.* **As verb,** هم **expresses the action of** *being disturbed,* **of** *interfering,* **of bustling about to do a thing.**

הוּם **Action of** *exciting a tumult, making a noise,*

disturbing **with clamour, with an unexpected crash; every** *perturbation, consternation, trembling,* **etc.**

These roots are describing a unexpected and violent colliding of the tectonic plates under the seas, which caused a trembling (earthquake) and a tremulous agitation (tsunami) to ravage the earth. This caused a destructive number of seismic sea wave to pound the earth submerging it under water.

We can see from the former events recorded here for us in Genesis 1:1-3, that these ancient events describe many frightful calamities, which ravaged the earth prior to the placing of Adam and Eve in the garden of Yahweh. The earth is described in this ancient history to have become a desolated waste place, because of the wars and fighting here on earth at that time. This history shows us the atmosphere and the visible heavens were also destroyed in the beginning. The atmosphere was caused to rise further above the earth causing changes in the upper and lower atmosphere. The changes brought about extreme droughts, tornadoes, earthquakes,

Written by
Yibniyah Hawkins
5/27/2013

tsunamis, and hurricanes. These disturbances caused the earth to become submerge under water and the atmosphere to collapse allowing an extreme compression force to cause the earth to heat up. This heat was the catalysis for the major storms that ravages the earth, along with scorching heat that caused the surface of the earth to become desolate. This ancient history shows the earth was shaking so mightily that it moved the earth out its place, caused by the dramatic changes in the thermosphere-magnetosphere and the ionosphere.

In the beginning Yahweh is shown to have corrected three major issues important for all life on earth. When he began to renovated the earth the first things he corrected were the issues preventing the sun from shining on earth. The reader must remember the earth was brought to this state, after Yahweh had created it. The upper atmosphere is strongly influence by the sun. The ionosphere-magnetosphere and thermosphere are designed to filter the solar winds and cosmic radiation from scorching the surface of the earth. They caused the right amount of sun-light and radiation to come to the surface which makes life possible for us. We could not exist without these three areas of the upper atmosphere performing the function they were created to perform for the benefit of all life on earth. In the beginning when Yahweh commanded the earth to be renovated he corrected all the issues preventing the equal distribution of light from shining on earth. This involved the renovation of the expanse (firmament) he called Heaven. The last thing he is described to have renovated was the gathering of the waters into there respectful places, because the earth was submerged under the waters of the seas.

In Genesis 1:1-25 we have recorded for us not only the history concerning the renovation of the earth, but also the ordinances of heaven and earth are recorded for all nations of the earth. These ordinances deal with all the life giving functions of the heavens and the earth which we depend on for life. The life giving functions establish by ordinances were created for the benefit of all mankind. In Genesis 1:26 Yahweh charges mankind to guard and protect the things his finger has made, which he created for the benefit of mankind.

The former events reveal that on earth in an ancient time were destructive weapons that utilized the enormous energy residing in the atom. These weapons are

Written by
Yibniyah Hawkins
5/27/2013

recorded to have destroyed and ravaged cities causing the earth to become desolate- waste place. The technological advancement in destructive weapons grew gradual as sin came to a peak. They came to understand the power residing in the upper atmosphere and began to utilize the atmosphere for military purposes. These pursuits began to cause major disturbances in the earth. The Government of Peace is admonishing the nations at this time to consider the former events so they can prevent the recurrence of this ancient destruction from destroying the earth again.

Chapter Four

Evidence of Climate &Nuclear Destruction in Ancient Times

Yahweh through his anointed ones in the last days is warning the governments of man to consider their ways. We have entering a time "that has already been" this was inspired to be written for us in the following scriptures:

The thing that has been, it is that which shall be; and that which is done is that which shall be done (again): and there is nothing new under the sun. Is there any thing of which it may be said, See, this is new? It has been already of old time, which was before us. *There* is no ***remembrance of former things***; neither shall there be *any* remembrance of *things* that are to come with *those* that shall come after.

Eccl 1:9-11 (KJV)

Written by
Yibniyah Hawkins
5/27/2013

There is Nothing New Under the Sun

I know that, whatsoever Yahweh does, it shall be for ever: nothing can be added to it, or any thing taken from it. Yahweh acts and *man* will give him reverence. ***That which has been is now; and that which is to be has already been; and Yahweh requires and accounting of what is past.***

Eccl 3:14-15 (KJV)

The above scripture reveal that there is nothing new that has not already been in ancient times. This should make the reader understand that all things are working according to a plan that was put in motion from the beginning. The former things are what Yahweh through is wisdom allowed to play out here on earth to be later displayed to the whole universe as means to stop sin and death. The universe is also watching Yahweh bring forth his family who will rule the universe in total righteousness guiding all creation from sin which leads to death. Yahweh as the reader can see from the above scriptures "requires and accounting of what is past". The word past written in the Ecclesiastes 3:15 is found in Webster Dictionary with this meaning:

Past: Webster Dictionary page 544: 1. Of a former time; indicating a time or state gone by or an action completed or in progress at a former time. The past: past time, states or happenings.

This accounting is what the two witnesses are commanded to teach the nations to consider.

Let all the nations be gathered together, and let the people be assembled: who among them can declare this, and show us former things? Let them bring forth their witnesses, that they may be justified: or let them hear, and say, *It is* truth.

Isaiah 43:9 (KJV)

Produce your cause, says Yahweh; bring forth your strong *reasons*, says the King of Jacob. Let them bring *them* forth, and show us what shall happen: let them show

Written by
Yibniyah Hawkins
5/27/2013

the former things, what they *be*, that we may consider them, and know the latter end of them; or declare us things to come.

Who has declared from the beginning, that we may know? and former times, that we may say, *He is* righteous? Yes, *there is* none that shows, yes, *there is* none that declares, yes, *there is* none that hears your words.

Isaiah 41:21-22, 26 (KJV)

This accounting is designed to prevent the re-occurrence of the former events in this generation. In the above scripture Ecclesiastes 1:9 shows us "that which has already been, will be done again", **if the nations refuse to take heed to this warning**. The prophet Danyl was inspired to write concerning the nations entering this time called by him "the Ancient of Days".

I saw in the night visions, and, behold, *one* like the Son of man came with the clouds of heaven, and **came to the Ancient of days**, and they brought him near before him. And there was given him dominion, and glory, and a kingdom, that all people, nations, and languages, should serve him: his dominion *is* an everlasting dominion, which shall not pass away, and his kingdom *that* which shall not be destroyed.

Dan 7:13-14 (KJV)

 I beheld, and the same horn made war with the saints, and prevailed against them; ***until the Ancient of days came***, and judgment was given to the saints of the most High; and the time came that the saints possessed the kingdom.

Dan 7:21-22 (KJV)

The word "ancient" written in the above scriptures is from the Hebrew word:

עַתִּיק 'attîq <u><H6268</u>—from <u><H6275></u> (`athaq); *removed*, i.e. *weaned*; also ***antique***:
- ***ancient***, drawn.

—Strong's Concordance

Written by
Yibniyah Hawkins
5/27/2013

There is Nothing New Under the Sun

Notice the meaning of the word **"antique"** found in the above definition of the Hebrew word "attiq"

Antique: Webster Dictionary page 32: ancient, before 1. *__Of ancient times; old; antiquate; to continued from, resembling or adhering to the past; to put in an earlier state . Syn: antiquity__*

Antiquity: Webster Dictionary page 94: *Ancient times; former ages.*

This word "antique" is describing for us former events, which took place in the ancient of days shown here by Danyl to return in the last days. The time we are in now is shown to resemble an ancient time when the earth experience the former events that come to pass in the beginning. This show us the earth is moving into a time were once again it can become without form and void. Notice this in the following scriptures:

How long shall I see the standard, *and* hear the sound of the trumpet? For my people *is* foolish, they have not known me; they *are* foolish children, and they have no understanding: they *are* wise to do evil, but to do righteousness they have no knowledge. *__I beheld the earth, and, lo, it was without form, and void; and the heavens, and they had no light. I beheld the mountains, and, lo, they trembled, and all the hills moved violently to and fro. I beheld, and, lo, there was no man, and all the birds of the heavens fled. I beheld, and, lo, the fruitful place was a wilderness, and all the cities thereof were broken down at the presence of YAHWEH, and by his fierce anger (judgment).__* For thus says Yahweh, The whole land shall be desolate; yet will I not make a full end. For this shall the earth mourn, and the heavens above are black*__: because I have spoken it, I have purposed it, and will not repent; neither will I turn back from it.__*

Jer 4:21-28 (KJV)

Yeremyah the prophet is shown here in the above scripture to see the earth once again experience the same destruction it did in the beginning. *"The prophet Isayah also was inspired to show us the end of Yahweh's plan was predicted from the*

Written by
Yibniyah Hawkins
5/27/2013

beginning". The plan was formed on the basis of the events that occurred in an ancient time. Notice this in the following scripture

Have you not heard long ago I ***done this***; and ***from ancient times, that I have formed it?*** Now have I brought it to pass, that you should be one to lay waste defense cities *into* ruinous heaps.

Isaiah 37:26 (KJV)

Notice the meaning of the word "done" which is from the Hebrew word:

עָשָׂה 'āśâ <u><H6213></u>—a primitive root; to *do* or *make*, in the broadest sense and widest application (as follows):- appoint**, bring forth, (put in) execute (-ion),** exercise**, fashion**, + bring (come) to pass, perform, procure, provide, **ordain,** requite,

—Strong's Concordance

This should read *"**Have you not heard that long ago I fashion this.**"*

Notice the word **"from"** written in the Isaiah 37:26 is found in the Webster Dictionary

From: Webster Dictionary page 301: *Out of; with the person or thing as the source, etc; as facts learned from 7. Out of the possibility or use of.*

The word from is revealing to us, that out of the facts, and evidence gain from an ancient time period Yahweh fashion not only this event, but his entire plan of salvation. Notice this fact from the word **"formed"** written in Isaiah 37:26 is from the Hebrew word:

יָצַר yāṣar <u><H3335></u>—probably identical with <H3334> (yatsar) (through the ideal of *squeezing* into shape); ([compare <H3331> (yatsaʾ)]); ***to mould into a form***; especially as a *potter*; ***figurative to determine (i.e. form a resolution***):- × fashion, form, frame, ***purpose***. **Yatsar: to form, fashion; frequently used to describe Yahweh's creative activity; Yatsar is used to express "Yahweh's planning or preordaining" according to His divine purpose.**

There is Nothing New Under the Sun

— **The New Strong's Expanded Concordance of the Bible Red-Letter Edition James Strong,LL.D.,S.T.D. Contributions by John R. Kohlenberger, III**

יֵצֶר **yēṣer <H3336>—from <H3335> (yatsar); a *form*; figurative *conception (i.e. purpose)*:- frame, a *thing framed,* imagination, mind, work.**

—Strong's Concordance

The word formed is describing to us how Yahweh out of the former events allowed to take place here on earth he created a plan. Through this plan he has preordained all things according to the purpose of his plan of salvation. The former events predicted in an ancient time he used as a basis to form resolution to stop sin and death from consuming all creation. This plan of salvation is model according to the evidence Yahweh gather from the former events. The prophet Isaiah was inspired to write from these former events Yahweh has pre-ordained all things and is able to declare the end of his plan from the beginning.

Remember the former things of old: for I *am* Yahweh, and *there is* none else; *I am* Yahweh, and *there is* none like me, Declaring the end from the beginning, and from ancient times *the things* that are not *yet* done, saying, My counsel shall stand, and I will do all my pleasure (*plan*):

Isaiah 46:9-10 (KJV)

We see from the above scripture Isaiah is reiterating for us that from (out of) an ancient time Yahweh predict all things that will occur. He as we establish earlier in this work, is displaying this plan as a public exhibit of evidence gather from former events. He is proving we cannot live in peace, without the laws of peace to guide us.

Written by
Yibniyah Hawkins
5/27/2013

There is Nothing New Under the Sun

This time period of mans history was also understood by Yahshua our Savior who was inspired to predict the last days would be similar to the events that occurred in the beginning. Notice this in the following scriptures

For then shall be great tribulation, such as has not come to pass since ***the beginning of the world to this time, no, nor ever shall be.*** And except those days should be shortened, there should no flesh be saved: but for the elect's sake those days shall be shortened.

Matt 24:21-22 (KJV)

For *in* those days there will be tribulation***, such has not been since the beginning of the creation which Yahweh created until this time, nor ever shall be***. And unless Yahweh had shortened those days, no flesh would be saved; but for the elect's sake, whom He chosen, He has shortened the days.

Mark 13:19-20 (NKJV)

In Mark 13:19 we see that Yahshua is revealing the similarity of the last days (the end) with the events that occurred in the beginning. He also shows in the above verse Yahweh formed this tribulation to be similar to the events, but not exactly ending as the events in the beginning. We will see later he reveals to his disciples disturbance that will take place in both the heaven and the earth in this generation. These disturbances are similar to those we saw earlier that caused the earth to become without form and void causing also death and destruction to consume the earth in the beginning. ***"It is important we understand the earth does not need to experience this destruction again, but we must consider these former events and destroy all weapons of mass destruction"***. Notice Yahshua our Savior predicted in this generation we would see the powers in heaven shaken. Notice this in the following scriptures:

And there shall be **signs in the sun, and in the moon, and in the stars; and upon the earth distress of nations, with perplexity; the sea and the waves roaring;**

Written by
Yibniyah Hawkins
5/27/2013

There is Nothing New Under the Sun

Men's hearts failing them for fear, and for looking after those things which are coming on the earth*: for the powers of heaven shall be shaken*.

Luke 21:25-26 (KJV)

I beg all nations to take heed to the Savior predictions. We are experiencing at this time incredible signs in the sun, the moon, and in the stars. Yahshua also predicts in this generation we would see the "the sea and the waves roaring" this is describing the raging of the seas *(hurricanes)*. He also gives us the reason for these occurrences notice the following stated above: "for the powers of heaven shall be shaken".

The word *powers* written in Luke 21:26 are from the Geek and Hebrew words:

The word *powers* written in the scripture above is from the Greek word: δύναμις dynamis <u><G1411</u>— from <u><G1410></u> (dunamai); *force* (literal or figurative); specially miraculous *power* (usually by implication a *miracle* itself):- ability, mighty, power, strength, violence, might (wonderful) work. — Strong's Concordance

The word powers when transliterated back to the Hebrew is the word חַיִל ḥayil <u><H2428</u>— from <H2342> (chuwl); probably **a *force***, *strength*: ***- activity of (great power-forces).*** —Strong's Concordance:

The word heaven written in Luke 21:26 is from the Greek and Hebrew words:

<u>*οὐρανός ouranos <G3772>— perhaps from the same as <G3735> (oros) (through the idea of elevation); "the sky"; by extension heaven —Strong's Concordance*</u>

Written by
Yibniyah Hawkins
5/27/2013

שָׁמַיִם *shāmayim* <u>*<H8064>*</u>*—dual of an unused singular shameh, shaw-meh'; from an unused root meaning to be lofty;* <u>*the sky*</u> *(as aloft; the dual perhaps alluding to the visible arch in which the clouds move, as well as to the higher ether where the celestial bodies revolve) Shameh also means the atmosphere immediately surrounding the earth; the vast expanse through which the stars are moving through their courses— The New Strong's Expanded Concordance of the Bible Red-Letter Edition James Strong's contribution by John R. Kohlenberger,III*

Notice the word shaken also written in Luke21:26

The word *shaken* written in the above scripture is from the Greek word: σαλεύω saleuō <u><G4531</u>—Strong's Concordance: from <u><G4535></u> (salos); to *waver*, i.e. *agitate, rock,* or (by implication) *destroy;* **figurative to *disturb, incite*: - move, shake (together),** be shaken, <u>**stir up**</u>. <u>**(To shake *(disturb)* the natural forces of the heavens and the heavenly bodies).**</u>

Yahshua is showing us in this last generation the natural forces of the atmosphere will be disturb, just as they were in the beginning. The atmospheric disturbances produce devastating storms <u>***(hurricanes, tornadoes, earthquakes)***</u> **that ravage the earth in the beginning, and will do the same in this generation if we do not heed the warning from the Kingdom of Heaven.**

Written by
Yibniyah Hawkins
5/27/2013

Chapter Five

An Accounting of What is Past

This brings me to a history that we have documented in secular history, which proves the earth in a ancient time period experience destruction similar to a nuclear explosion. This history is documented in one the oldest nations on this earth today "India." The information we will provide will make clear what many scientist and historians are in agreement with, **<u>the earth has experience a form of nuclear destruction in the past</u>**. In a book entitle " Mysteries From Forgotten World" by Charles Berlitz he describes from the research of geologists, paleontologists, pre-historians, and astronomers the earth has experience cataclysmic changes. The research he and other have conducted describes the massive changes to the surface of the earth, the extermination of its human and animal populations, change its climate zones, push up its mountains, raised lands from the sea, and sunk other lands beneath the oceans. The evidence of a catastrophic planet-wide destruction is shown in some remarkable discoveries over the years. Early Russian explores documented in northern Siberia they found masses of bones of elephants, rhinoceroses and other animals wedged so close together that they formed hills. Professor Immanuel Velikovsky a historian and astronomer describes in his work catastrophic destruction in an ancient time in his book "Worlds in Collision" Notice this in the following information:

> ➢ *In the hills of Montreal and New Hampshire and in Michigan, five and six hundred feet above sea level, bones of whales have been found. In many places on the earth-on all continents- bones of sea animals and polar land*

Written by
Yibniyah Hawkins
5/27/2013

animals and tropical animals have been found in great melees; so also in Cumberland Cave in Maryland in the Chou Kou Tien fissures in China, and in Germany and Denmark. Hippopotamuses and ostriches were found together with seals and reindeer… from the Arctic and Antarctic…in high mountains and in the deep seas- we found innumerable signs of great upheavals, ancient and recent….. Worlds in Collison…..

The historians have documented evidence that man didn't disappear as a result of these catastrophes, but they went temporally "underground" taking shelter in caves or on hilltops. These survivors from all over the world were able to relay their experiences to succeeding generations of the destruction by fire, ice, earthquakes and sinking's in great details. In one of the Aztec Codices, the codex of Chimalpopoca describes a recurring catastrophe notice this from the Codex Chimalpopoca:

> *The third sun is called Quia-Tonatiuh, sun of rain, because there fell a rain of fire; all which existed burned; and there fell a rain of gravel. They also relate that while the sandstone, which we now see scattered about, and the tetzontli (basaltic rock) boiled with great tumult, there also rose the rocks of vermilion color…. Now in this day, in which men are lost and destroyed in a rain of fire; the sun itself was on fire, and everything, together with the houses, was consumed…… Aztec Codices…*

There are many ancient sources that document the earth has experience fire, destruction, darkness, earthquakes and the "erratic behavior of planets in ancient times. The scriptures alone with secular history documents the repeated changes in the earth's orbit, the inclination of its axis and changes in the seasons and the year. It also shows there were hurricanes of global magnitude, stones and ashes falling from the sky, and boiling seas. The scripture shows periodic adjustment in the polarity of the earth affecting its rotation or solar orbit. There were many abnormalities due to the magnetic tension and stress built up within this enormous generator we call earth. This caused violent modifications of the earth's climate, surface, and atmosphere in the past. It is evident as the scripture shows we stand at

Written by
Yibniyah Hawkins
5/27/2013

this moment with the technological advancement we have to modify for good or evil the environment we depend on for life. There is a reference in many ancient writings of the use of "crystals" in ancient warfare, were they unleash the power of the crystals at the atomic level.

This leads me to an ancient source of history the Ramayana and Mahabharata (c. 1000-500 BC) they focused on conflicts and refer to military formations, warfare and "esoteric weaponry". The "Mahabharata" also known as the Iliad of ancient India began to be study by the western world in the period of British rule in India. The reader must understand the "Mahabharata" was written thousand of years before the atomic bomb and other technological advancements of our time. The Mahabharata gives detailed references to ancient air ships (vimanas) including instruction on how to construct them, how to power the air ships (vimanas). It also gave descriptions of controlled fire power in warfare, rockets and even what they called the ***"arrow of unconsciousness" (mohanastra).*** The early western scholar perceived this description as none sense until the invention of the airplane and the atomic bomb. Dr. Robert J. Oppenhimer the inventor of the atomic weapon that was detonated July 16, 1945 is in a documentary recorded after the explosion were he quoted from the "Mahabharata," that he and the other scientists have become "the destroyers of worlds". It is know fact he and others study this ancient text and it was the motivating factor in the creation of the atomic bomb.

The Mahabharata was a very strange and mysterious text to the early scholars who read and study text. The description of total warfare and carnage can be understood today by this generation who witness the start of the "Atomic Age". The reader can judge for themselves the incredible details that are astonishingly familiar today despite thousands of intervening years when this account actual occurred. The prophets were inspired to write for us "that which has already been done, is what will yet be done again" if we do not heed the warning. Notice the following experts from "the Mahabharata" (English Translation)-Protap- Chandra, Roy-Calcutta 1889.

Written by
Yibniyah Hawkins
5/27/2013

There is Nothing New Under the Sun

> ➢ *A single projectile charged with all the power of the Universe. An incandescent column of smoke and flame, as bright s ten thousand Suns, rose in all its splendor*

> ➢ *.... it was an unknown weapon, an __"iron thunderbolt"__ a gigantic messenger of death which reduced to ashes the entire race of the Vrishnis and the Andhakas.*

> ➢ *..... The corpses were so burned as to be unrecognizable. Their hair and nails fell out; pottery broke without any apparent cause, and the birds turned white. After a few hours, all foodstuffs were infected.*

> ➢ *..... to escape from this fire the soldiers threw themselves in streams to wash themselves and all their equipment..... (The Mahabharata)*

Remember earlier in this work (subject concerning Rahab and the dragon) I ask the reader to remember this weapon describe by Isaiah the prophet as **the ("Iron thunderbolt of the gods").** Here we see it mention in the Mahabharata which describes a war that occurred in an ancient time. It is also describe in another work notice this following information:

> ➢ *.... "Then Vayu (the presiding deity of that mighty weapon) bore away crowds of Samsaptakas with steeds and elephants and cars and weapons, as if these were dry leaves of trees...... Borne away by the wind, O King, they looked highly beautiful like flying birds.....flying away from trees...." (Samsaptaka-Badha Parva of the Drona Parva)*

Notice the following in another source:

> ➢ *"Meteors flashed down from the firmament.... A thick gloom suddenly shrouded the host. All points of the compass were enveloped by that darkness.... Inauspicious winds began to blow..... the sun seemed to turn*

around, the universe, scorched with heat, seems to be in a fever. The elephants and other creatures of the land, scorched by the energy of that weapon, ran in flight.... The very water being heated, the creatures residing in that element began to burn..... hostile warriors fell down like trees burnt down in a raging fire-huge elephants burnt by that weapon, fell down on the earth....uttering fierce cries....other(s) scorched by the fire ran hither and thither, as in the midst of a forest conflagration, the steeds.... And the cars (chariots) also, burnt by the energy of that weapon looked.... Like the top of trees burnt in a forest fire..... (Naryanastra Mokshana Parva (Drona Parva)

If the above was not enough to convince you let me take you in deeper into this nuclear war:

- ➤ *"It was a weapon) so powerful that it could destroy the earth*
  in an instant A great soaring sound in smoke and flames
  And on its sits death..." – The Ramayana
- ➤ *"Dense arrows of flame, like a great shower, issued*
  forth upon creation, encompassing the enemy...
  A thick gloom swiftly settled upon the Pandava hosts.
  All points of the compass were lost in darkness.
  Fierce wind began to blow upward, showering dust and gravel.
- ➤ *Birds croaked madly... the very elements seemed disturbed.*
  The earth shook, scorched by the terrible violent heat of this weapon.
  Elephants burst into flame and ran to and fro in frenzy...
  over a vast area, other animals crumpled to the ground and died.
  From all points of the compass the arrows of flame rained
  continuously and fiercely. — The Mahabharata

- ➤ *"Fires, when ignited, cast their flames towards the left. Sometimes they threw out flames*
  whose splendor was blue and red. The Sun, whether when rising or setting
  over the city,

Written by
Yibniyah Hawkins
5/27/2013

There is Nothing New Under the Sun

seemed to be surrounded by headless trunks of human form. In cook rooms, upon food that
was clean and well-boiled, were seen, when it was served out for eating, innumerable
worms of diverse kinds."----- The Mahabharata

Notice the following after effects document for us:

> *....winds dry and strong and showering gravel blew from every side.... Birds began to wheel making circles.... The horizon on every sides seemed to be covered with fog. Meteors-showering blazing coals fell on the earth from the sky..... The Sun's disk .... Seemed to be always covered with dust..... Fierce circles of light were seen every day around both the sun and the moon.... A little while after the Kuru King, Yudhishshira heard of the wholesale carnage of the Vrishnis in consequences of the "**iron thunderbolt.....** (Mausala Parva)*

This ancient history also describes the composition of both earth and the atmosphere undergoing change forming destructive layers of heat waves and electrical charge rays. The cloud of electrical charge rays and heat could be concentrate over any region of the earth creating huge layers of heat waves above the earth. The electrically charge rays and heat would fall to earth having been charged by the upper atmosphere causing unthinkable destruction on the surface of the earth.

Written by
Yibniyah Hawkins
5/27/2013

Reestablishing the Past

The earth today is facing the same type of destruction because of the technological advancements of the nations today. They have also developed similar technology that existed in ancient times. The governments today have also learned about the enormous power existing in the upper atmosphere, and how it can be use for military purposes. They have not understood the destructive effects these pursuits will have on the earth, but they have continued to develop advance weaponry designed to gain control of the power in the upper atmosphere. Let's review some of the information proving the nations have pursued this power for about seventy years.

> *Meteorologist Harry Wexler had little patience for those who wanted to add weather and climate modification to the set of tools in man's possession. But by 1958 even he acknowledged that serious proposals for massive changes, using nuclear weapons as tools, were inevitable. Like most professional meteorologists, in the past he had dismissed the idea that hydrogen bombs had affected the weather. But with the prospect of determined experiments designed to bring about such changes, he warned of "the unhappy situation of the cure being worse than the ailment."*

> *Whatever one might have thought about the wisdom of tinkering with the weather in peacetime, the manipulation of nature on a vast scale for military purposes seemed to be a perfectly legitimate application of scientific knowledge. While planning a total war against the Soviet Union, every avenue begged for exploration. Let's explore how the scientific advisors of America's key allies in NATO saw the alliance fighting in the future. Numerous ideas for creating catastrophic events through natural processes were presented, especially using hydrogen bombs as triggers. In these discussions, held as early as 1960, top scientists debated the fundamental*

Written by
Yibniyah Hawkins
5/27/2013

environmental question — can humans have a long-term effect on the global environment? <u>**"Arming Mother Nature: The Birth of Catastrophic Environmentalism"**</u>

President Eisenhower formed a special committee for the study of weather modification who presented a special report in January 1958. This committee's chairman Navy Captain Howard T. Orville gave a press conference were he stated "the Soviet Union has already begun secret programs for weather control". Mr. Orville urged the government to support research in controlling weather systems. He suggested the military finds ways to manipulate the heat balance between the sun and the earth as means to control the climate. President Eisenhower created a science advisory committee to guide the progress of United States government technology. The President Science Advisory Committee (PSAC) establishes an elite group of scientists who studied major scientific and technological research for military purposes. In the same time frame the Soviet Union launch the Sputnik in October 1957, it reorganized military strategy, this lead to the summoning of military planners by NATO who discussed weather modification for war. Notice this in the following information

➢ *Thus in late 1962, NATO summoned scientists and military planners to Paris to hammer out what might legitimately come out of "environmental warfare" and what the long-term consequences might be. The central question almost always remained the same: were natural forces susceptible to human influence on a large, even global, scale?* <u>**In methodical fashion, these military planners broke down environmental warfare into distinct spheres of possibility, corresponding with the layers of the earth and its atmosphere as it extended into space: lithosphere and hydrosphere (land and oceans), troposphere (lower atmosphere), stratosphere and ionosphere (upper atmosphere), and exosphere (outer space)**</u>. <u>*"Arming Mother Nature: The Birth of Catastrophic Environmentalism"*</u>

Written by
Yibniyah Hawkins
5/27/2013

There is Nothing New Under the Sun

NATO focused its attention on an area in outer space called the "exosphere". They saw great results could be obtained from the radiation belts that surround the earth. These belts are called the "Van Allen Belts" they are regions of extremely charged particles trapped in the earth's magnetic field. The belts could be used as an intense source of radiation destroying anything in its path. The United States government came to the understanding that they could artificially create these belts by exploding nuclear or thermo-nuclear weapons at an altitude of 400 kilometers or higher. These artificial belts would cloak the earth creating layers of heat and layers of electrical charge particles in both the north and south geomagnetic poles.

Through a project called "ARGUS" the United States discovered by exploding nuclear bombs in the upper atmosphere they could create electron shells around the earth, this was called the "ARGUS" effect. The United States went even further in another project called the "Starfish Experiment" they detonated larger bombs at even greater altitudes. This created an enormous amount of electrons that were trapped in the earth's magnetic field forming "New Van Allen Belts." These belts were greater in electron density than all the known Van Allen belts that surround the earth.

The above information shows us we are following in the same path of destruction that destroyed the earth in the beginning. The ancient nations developed the ability to utilize the earth atmosphere for military purpose vowing to never use this technology in war. The nations today deny the knowledge of such technology to control the weather are to use the atmosphere to cause destruction far greater then any nuclear explosion. The governments involved in this form of research should ask themselves can we afford to deny or disregard the destructive effects of our inventions any longer. There is only one, Yahweh, who can see the future. And he is admonshing the nations at this time to consider the former events that took place here on earth. Notice this in the following scriptures:

Yahweh will lay bare *(reveal)* his holy arm in the eyes *(sight)* of all the nations; and all the ends of the earth shall see the salvation of our Father.

Written by
Yibniyah Hawkins
5/27/2013

There is Nothing New Under the Sun

Behold, my servant shall deal prudently, he shall be exalted and extolled, and be very high. Just as many were astonished at you; his visage was so marred more than any man, and his form more than the sons of men: So shall he sprinkle many nations; ***the kings shall shut their mouths at him: for that which had not been told them shall they see; and that which they had not heard shall they consider.***

Isaiah 52:10, 13-15 (KJV)

Speak out, and bring *your proofs near*; yes, let them take counsel together: who has declared this from ancient time? *Who* has told it from that time? *Have* not I Yahweh? And *there is* no source of power beside me; a just Father and a Saviour; *there is* none beside me. Look unto me, and be saved, all the ends of the earth: for I *am* Yahweh, and *there is* none else.

Isaiah 45:21-22 (KJV)

Who has performed and done *it,* calling the generations from the beginning? I, Yahweh, the first, and I will be with the last; I *am* he.

Isaiah 41:4 (KJV)

Come near to me, hear this***; I have not spoken in secret from the beginning***; *from the time that it was, there am I*: And now Father Yahweh has sent me with his Spirit.

Isaiah 48:16 (KJV)

The nations today are admonished by Yahweh to bring forth their strong reasons against the former things he has commanded to be remembered. The nations are also admonished by him to assembly and counsel together to consider, and prove for themselves the former events which he predicted actually come to pass.

Written by
Yibniyah Hawkins
5/27/2013

There is Nothing New Under the Sun

Yahweh shows he caused to remain as evidence of these former events visible indications of the destruction in both the heavens and the earth. I ask the nations today to heed the words of the great prophet Isaiah which he was inspired to write in the following scripture.

Come now, and let us reason together, says Yahweh: though your sins are as scarlet, they shall be as white as snow; though they be red like crimson, they shall be as wool. If you are willing and obedient, you shall eat the fruit of the land: ***But if you refuse and rebel, you shall be devoured with the sword: for the mouth of Yahweh has spoken.***

>   Isaiah 1:18-20 (KJV)

The prophet Yeremyah was inspired to write for us concerning the prophets in an ancient time that prophesied of destruction, and warned the government at that time about. Notice this in the following scripture

The prophets that have been before me and before you of ***old prophesied both against many countries, and against great kingdoms, of war, and of evil, and of pestilence.***

Jer 28:8 (KJV)

The word "old" is from the Hebrew word:

עוֹלָם 'ôlām <H5769> or *olam*, o-lawm'; from <H5956> (`alam); properly *concealed*, i.e. the *vanishing* point; generally time *out of mind* (past or future), i.e. Frequent adverb (especially with prepositional prefix) **ancient (time), of old)**, long (time), (of) old (time), (beginning of the) world Olam: ***at the very beginning*——** Strong's Concordance

Written by
Yibniyah Hawkins
5/27/2013

עוֹלָם ʻôlām: found in the Gensenius's Hebrew and Chaldee Lexicon by Samuel Tregelles page 612

עוֹלָם sometimes עֹלָם m.—(A) pr. what is hidden; specially *hidden time, long;* the beginning or end of which is either uncertain or else not defined; *eternity, perpetuity.* It is used—(1) of *time long past,* antiquity, in the following phrases and examples, יְמֵי עוֹלָם Am. 9:11; Mic. 7:14; Isa. 63:9; and יְמוֹת עוֹלָם Deu. 32:7, ancient times. מֵעוֹלָם *of old, from the most ancient times,* Gen. 6:4; 1 Sa. 27:8; Isa. 63:16; Jer. 2:20; 5:15; Ps. 25:6; and even of time before the creation of the world [i. e. eternity],

The above information proves that Yahweh from the very beginning had prophets warning the nations to avoid the destruction they were bringing on themselves. I admonish all nations today to consider the former things and to believe what is written for our learning. History seems to remind us of our repetitive behavior and continues to warn us of our on self –destruction, because we refuse to learn from and embrace history. I will end this work with a well known French saying which deserves our attention and devotion. "Those who ignore history are doomed to repeat it"

A generous, open hearted and Princely man writes on all his possession for myself and for mankind.

Written by
Yibniyah Hawkins
5/27/2013

There is Nothing New Under the Sun

Yibniyah Hawkins

Eyes on the Truth

Written by
Yibniyah Hawkins
5/27/2013

There is Nothing New Under the Sun

Written by
Yibniyah Hawkins
5/27/2013